"Finally, a book about women succeeding in business without sacrificing their health or their families!"
~Cornelia van der Ziel, M.D., OB/GYN, FACOG
Harvard University Medical School Clinical Instructor
Co-Author, Big, Beautiful and Pregnant (Avalon, 2006)

"When life seems full of impossible hurdles, sometimes just hearing an inspiring story of how someone else overcame great adversity to achieve great things can motivate us to continuously fight for our dreams. Kathleen's book, *Climbing the Corporate Ladder in High Heels*, is full of these kinds of real-life stories, including my own story of how I spent 3 months rowing single-handedly across the Atlantic after my partner had to be rescued. But this book is not just a book of stories. It is full of practical advice and exercises to help you make those dreams a reality in more than just your career, but in life, as well."
~Debra Veal, BBC Television Presenter
and (Transatlantic) Atlantic Rower

"Kathleen Archambeau weaves some of the studies we've conducted at Carnegie Mellon into a practical set of guidelines for women who are attempting to move beyond their proscribed gender roles to actualize their highest potential. *Climbing the Corporate Ladder in High Heels* honors those traditional gender roles, while showing women how to take those roles forward for success in business and in life."
~Linda C. Babcock, Ph.D.
Co-Author of bestseller, *Women Don't Ask*
(Princeton University Press, 2003)
James Mellon Walton Professor of Economics,
Carnegie Mellon University

"Kathleen's chapter on *The Cheerleader* captures the philosophy I learned as a student at the university where I now chair the Board of Trustees: 'Give THEM the Credit.' Much success in life flows from recognizing the contributions of our colleagues and associates along the way."

~Carol Corrigan, JD
Chairman of the Board
St. Vincent's Day Home, formerly, Holy Names University
Endorsing as a private citizen and fellow board member
Voted Judge of the Year in California (2004)
Appointed to the California Supreme Court (2005)

"*Climbing the Corporate Ladder in High Heels* breaks new ground. After 20 years of working with women corporate executives and professionals, I can tell you that this book will shock you and help you change the way you work and play. No other book for women trying to succeed in Corporate America presents quite this idea of reaching a pinnacle of financial security and creative expression, while keeping most of the central aspects of your life intact. No other book tells you quite how to do it. Not only does Ms. Archambeau tell you how to do it, but she delivers real-world examples from her real-work 20 years of corporate life experience."

~Nicole Schapiro
San Francisco Immigrant of the Year in 1997
NY Times Featured Author,
Negotiating for Your Life (Henry Holt, 1997)

"*Climbing the Corporate Ladder in High Heels* is not an 'in your face' attack on men. Instead, it is a realistic guide to politically navigating the world of Corporate America. It is about time women learned the secrets to success that will assure them the financial rewards and personal satisfaction that have eluded so many. As a corporate executive, I'd give the same advice Kathleen gives to any woman trying to strike a balance between the personal and the professional."

~Jack Biggane
Former U.S. Vice President of Sales and Self-Made
Millionaire, Verisign, Inc.

Climbing the Corporate Ladder
in High Heels

by

Kathleen Archambeau

CAREER
PRESS

Franklin Lakes, NJ

CLIMBING THE CORPORATE LADDER IN HIGH HEELS
EDITED BY DIANNA WALSH
TYPESET BY ASTRID DERIDDER
Cover design by Lu Rossman/Digi Dog Design
Printed in the U.S.A. by Book-mart Press

To order this title, please call toll-free 1-800-CAREER-1 (NJ and Canada: 201-848-0310) to order using VISA or MasterCard, or for further information on books from Career Press.

CAREER
PRESS

The Career Press, Inc., 3 Tice Road, PO Box 687,
Franklin Lakes, NJ 07417
www.careerpress.com

Library of Congress Cataloging-in-Publication Data

Archambeau, M. Kathleen.
    Climbing the corporate ladder in high heels / by Kathleen Archambeau.
        p. cm.
    Includes bibliographical references.
    ISBN-13: 978-1-56414-876-6
    ISBN-10: 1-56414-876-9 (pbk.)
        1. Women executives. 2. Career development. 3. Success in business. 4. Work and family. I. Title.

HD6054.3.A73 2006
658.4′09082—dc22

2006040185

Dedication

To all the women who want
a career and a life.
This book's for you.

And to my mom,
who would have been so proud.

Acknowledgments

I would like to thank my agent, Elizabeth Pomada, from the Larsen-Pomada Literary Agency, who helped me take this book in a new direction. Thanks to Chris Berg, who led me to Mike Larsen, who led me to Elizabeth.

This book would not have borne fruit without the creative work and support of colleagues, including Cindy Hegger, Allen Rice, Marduk Sayad, Barbara Wichmann, and Victoria Zackheim. Thanks to Pat Tompkins, my editorial conscience. My wonderful writing group of the past 10 years, Bella Brigada in San Francisco, remain my companions on this sometimes solitary journey. All the readers and endorsers of the book have touched my life in significant and memorable ways, for which I am grateful. Early adopters—Fr. Seamus Genovese, Laurie Ridgeway, May Wolff, Rhonda Chiljan, Beth Ramos, Elizabeth Breslin, Laura Atkins, Diane Davidson, Lisa Friedman, Thea Farhadian, Jacqueline Berg, Pam David, Rhea Feldman, and David Bergen, Sr. Joan Clark, Dr. Susie Kisber, Dr. Daniel Roth, Liz Rigali, Simao Avila, Anna Marks, Lori Hope, Rose Castillo Guilbault, Mindy and Bruce Bowles, Nicole Schapiro, Laila Svendsen, and Caroline and Ed Monie—stayed with me throughout the process. Sisters Annette, Lili, Michelle, and Nora, and friends, you know who you are, all buoyed my spirits.

Michael Pye, the senior acquisitions editor, led the Career Press team in supporting my work, along with Astrid deRidder and Dianna Walsh, editors, Linda Rienecker, publicity, and Ron Fry, publisher. Career Press has proven to be all that a small press should be—nurturing, guiding, encouraging, and celebrating the author. Their professionalism is unparalleled.

Foremost on this journey has been my beloved, whose constancy, love, and support made the journey, as well as the reward, sweet.

Contents

Introduction

There are 63 million working women in America and only 1.6 percent Fortune 500 CEOs (*National Association of Female Executives*, 2005). Though women make up nearly 50 percent of the workforce, working women with families perform more than 90 percent of the household and childcare duties (Hochschild, 2003). More than 40 percent of corporate women professionals over 40 never marry or have children (Hewlett, 2002) Women wonder, "Has my life become all work and no play?" This book is for you. This book answers the question: "How can I have it all?"

You should be able to have a job *and* have a life. "In a civilized society, no one should have to choose between a job and a life" (Freely in Greer, 2000). You don't have to lose weight. You don't have to change your hair. You don't have to alter your communication style. You don't have to mimic the male buttoned-down suit to dress for success. All you have to do is use your natural talents to succeed in business and in life. This book identifies 12 traditional female roles, many or all of which you have all performed, and shows how you can use the skills garnered in those roles to have a rewarding career *and* a happy life.

French Women Don't Get Fat (Guiliano, 2005) because they work a 35-hour week and have a two-hour lunch every day, not just because their food is mostly natural and unprocessed and they eat small portions. Despite this balanced approach, or maybe because of it, the French are among the most productive in the world (Forbes.com, 2005). Balance is the goal of the Soccer Mom in Chapter 2.

Neither the "break through the glass ceiling" school of thought nor the "sugar and spice and everything nice" little girl approach, this book tells women how to be both successful and fulfilled without becoming just like men.

From the Princess to the Soccer Mom, from the Cheerleader to the Athlete, from the Socialite to the Soul Sister, from the Psychic to the Apprentice, from the Girl Scout to the Diva, and from the Chef to the CEO, you will find yourself in these pages. From the famous to the unheralded, you will hear stories of how to make it on your own terms.

With practical exercises at the end of every chapter, you'll learn:

- ❖ How to climb the corporate ladder and have fun doing it.
- ❖ How to use 12 of your natural roles and talents to advance in Corporate America.
- ❖ How to thrive in a downsizing and outsourcing global economy.
- ❖ The secret of becoming a billionaire.

❖ How to achieve both success and joy.

❖ What to do when you hit the glass ceiling.

This book is dedicated to you. You deserve to advance in your career and enjoy your life. In a time of corporate scandal and bankruptcies, wars and terrorism, isn't it time you stop looking to the male model of success? Isn't it time you trust your own instincts about what it means to be successful? Isn't it time you redefine what it means to climb the corporate ladder?

Chapter 1

Kiss the princes. Lose the frogs.

The Princess

*The trouble with being in the rat race is
that even if you win, you're still a rat.*

~ Lily Tomlin
actress and comedienne

The Fairy Tale

Once upon a time, there lived a beautiful princess. A wicked witch, jealous of her blonde hair, creamy skin, and awesome beauty, cast a spell on her. In the king's castle, the princess was condemned to a long sleep and could only be awakened by the kiss of a prince. Her father paraded young men from throughout the kingdom before her, but only when the true prince came did the princess awaken.

There are many froggy companies out there where women are relegated to support roles or sex symbols. There is little hope of advancement and even slimmer chance for professional recognition. For women, only a prince of a company can awaken your potential. The froggy companies keep you trapped in a sleep of unrealized talents and dreams. But how do you find a prince among so many frogs?

Your First Company

There is a scene in the movie *Moonstruck* where Olympia Dukakis turns down the overtures of a professor in a restaurant. Sitting alone after just finding out that her husband of 30 years has cheated on her, she says, "I can't invite you in because I'm married. Because I know who I am." The first step to finding the right company for you is to know who you are. Know your roots and your core values before signing up for a company that may not share them.

Growing up in an Irish-Catholic extended family, I knew who I was as a person. My first company was made up of raconteurs and poets, cable-car operators and sheriffs on horses. One pacifist uncle got out of the service during World War II by claiming to be color blind, only to come home to drive a cab in San Francisco. His beliefs about peace were more important to him than being perceived as patriotic.

My grandmother was near Valencia Street at 5:12 the morning of the Great Earthquake on April 18, 1906. When I asked her, "Gram, what were you doing out at that hour?" She replied, "We told our mother we had to work late, tying up brown-wrapped packages until five in the morning. Instead, my sisters and I went out dancing all night!" That may have been what spared them the fires that ravaged the city following the earthquake. Having a good time was a basic value that showed up again in my grandmother's kitchen, when she kicked up her black orthopedic high heels and lifted her jersey dress in a mean Irish jig at the age of 80.

From my grandmother, I also learned to move on. When I was in fifth grade, she began taking me to the funerals of her many friends, where I observed her laughing and crying and telling stories. Following the Rosary for the family of friends of the deceased at the Irish wakes, she would grab my hand and take me on the bus headed downtown for shopping at the Emporium and dinner at the Ramona Hotel on Powell Street.

The lap of my first company taught me how to enjoy life, to value and respect people of all ages and lifestyles, to do what you feel is right no matter what anybody else thinks, and to move on even if your best friend dies. The light of the Moran family casts a long shadow, reminding me of the motto on our family crest: *Lucent en tenebris*. (In darkness, they shine their light.) The light of my first company has guided all my associations since.

The Company You Keep

"You shall know them by the company they keep," the Sisters of Mercy intoned. In 2005, Hewlett-Packard (HP) was chosen the best of the Top 25 companies by the Professional Businesswomen of California for the third year in a row. The National Association of Female Executives named HP number five of its Top 30 Companies for Executive Women (*NAFE*, 2004). Because of the 40 percent of women participants in an accelerated development program and, more importantly, the fact that women hold two of the five top P&L jobs, it is not surprising that HP tops every list of companies for women. That's why when I decided to join my first corporation in the early 1980s, I chose Hewlett-Packard. Quickly, HP proved its commitment to women's advancement by allowing two women to job-share one of the highest-ranking P&L positions at the company, general manager. The two women each worked three days a week, two independently, and one overlapping. That computer systems division was one of the most profitable divisions in the company that year. Early on, Hewlett-Packard led the way in enlightened work-life balance policies that favored women's success.

When I first started at HP, I was working on the division newsletter for an integrated circuits division with 24/7 operations. It was 6:30 p.m. and I was writing a story, frankly, not looking forward to the prospect of going home to my empty apartment when my boss came around to my cubicle. "Get out of here. It's 6:33! Time to call it a day. You'll have a lot more to offer if you go home and refresh yourself with friends and other activities." So, dutifully and reluctantly, I packed up my briefcase and headed home. I wound up playing tennis with a college friend and sipping jasmine tea at her house nearby. That boss was right. His admonition pushed me to balance my work with my personal life and kept me from falling into the workaholic trap early on in my career.

Value Matters

Probably the first way to discern a prince from a frog is to observe his behavior, not the mission statement on the walls of the corporate headquarters or the clichés handed down by senior executives at company quarterly meetings.

To find a prince of a company, find a company that aligns with your own personal values. If you value family and community and your company rewards long hours and "face time" after hours, think twice about accepting that lucrative offer of a big salary and stock options. My brother-in-law found this out the hard way. He usually left the office at 6:30 p.m. to go home to his wife and two daughters for dinner; he was laid off shortly after being hired for not having the "energy and commitment" the company was looking for in its IT staff. At 40, he already felt "over the hill" because he wasn't sticking around for the 10 p.m. pizza and foosball parties that were "au courant" at the consulting firm. Today, he works for a company that encourages family life and maintains reasonable work schedules to prove it. Ironically, it's a company headed by a woman, World Savings.

If you value integrity, and the company has a history of environmental or financial abuses, move on to your next prospect. One lawyer and CPA was blackballed from the biotech industry for "blowing the whistle" on research grant abuses at a major university. Though he won the case three years after signaling the abuse, the settlement did not make up for the three years of lost income and stymied career opportunities.

If you value people and relationships, and the company wooing you has quantified every minute of every day into productivity units, you're probably in the wrong place. One telephone company utility worker started having heart palpitations when the Texas firm that took over her local telecom company began reducing the workforce and tripling the number of pole climb calls required regardless of travel time from job site to job site.

If you value making money, make sure the company you choose ties compensation to performance and not to such superfluous criteria as politics, participation in team-building activities, titles, or tenure. One radio advertising account executive was offered a commission-only sales job and she took it, out-performing by more than $100,000 all her colleagues who were paid base salary plus commission.

"Birds of a Feather Flock Together"

Every year, the National Association of Female Executives, *Working Mother* magazine, Moskowitz and Levering in *Fortune* magazine, and the Professional Businesswomen of California cite the best companies for women. Every year, many of the same names come up on the list.

IBM, the largest company on NAFE Top 30 companies for Executive Women (NAFE, 2004), has a women's workforce of

30 percent, with 23 percent of its women in management. Never satisfied with anything less than the best, IBM has instituted a Global Women's Council to identify women prospects for all its succession plans.

Companies who make these "best" lists year after year enjoy the presence of women in essential executive positions and, more importantly, programs that identify high-potential women and put them on the fast track to top-earner positions. Women-friendly companies are child-friendly companies, often paying for childcare for overnight business travel and hosting childcare facilities on site or nearby. Companies committed to women boast women's councils, formal mentoring and networking programs, leadership development training courses, and annual professional women's conferences. Women-friendly cultures give additional paid family leave and extended part-time work with full benefits to returning mothers.

The 2005 Professional Business Women of California presented 25 Bay Area companies with its Pacesetter Awards based on the following positive criteria:

- ❖ Percentage of women corporate officers

- ❖ Percentage of women directors on the board

- ❖ Percentage of women employees

- ❖ Percentage of women executives defined as vice president or equivalent and above

- ❖ Development and continuing support of programs that benefit women in the workplace

Some of the same companies appear every year. Gap, Inc., led by several women division presidents, leads the way in retail. Guidant brings cardiac and vascular technology to market, with an emphasis on the growing numbers of women with heart disease. Genentech secured FDA approval for four new drugs under the aegis of an African-American woman president of commercial operations. Hewlett-Packard, SBC, Bank of America, Schwab, AT&T, Sun Microsystems, ChevronTexaco, and McKesson make the "best" lists nearly every year.

The Best for Moms

Every October, *Working Mother* magazine, published by the National Association of Female Executives, identifies the 100 Best Companies for Women. Companies were also selected as the Best in Class in the following categories vital to working women with children in 2004:

Representation of Women:

Liz Clairborne, Inc.: More than 75 percent of LCI's workforce is women, with 79 percent managers, 64 percent executives, and 51 percent corporate executives. Two of 10 corporate governing board members are women.

Advancing Women:

Booz Allen Hamilton: Female attendance at mentoring and career counseling programs reached 4,637 last year, with 3,710 women attending management/leadership training, support groups, and advancement conferences and forums.

Total Compensation:

JPMorgan Chase: Of the top earners at JPMorgan, 31 percent are women. New moms get full pay for the entire 12 weeks of FMLA leave. Moms who adopt get the same benefits and a $10,000 adoption fee reimbursement. The company offers discounted employee stock purchase plans, tuition reimbursement, and scholarships for employees' children.

Childcare:

IBM Corporation: IBM sponsors 63 full-time on- or near-site childcare centers, serving 2,324 employee children. Company-sponsored childcare includes before- and after-school care, family childcare homes, and summer programs. The childcare resource and referral service was used by 12,219 employees in 2003.

Flexibility:

S.C. Johnson & Son, Inc.: Last year, 64 percent of the S.C. Johnson workforce compressed their workweeks, 55 percent worked flextime, and 37 percent telecommuted.

Family-Friendly Company Culture:

Wachovia Corporation: Wachovia trained 2,178 managers on work/life issues and 2,083 on flex scheduling. More than 7,000 employees used the company's employee assistance program and another 6,053 used the elder-care resource and referral service.

Women of Color's Best Bet

Women of color face the added challenges of prejudice, negative stereotyping, economic disadvantage, and isolation as they climb to the top of corporations. But some companies are better than others when it comes to mining the talent pool of women of color. In 2003, when *Working Mother* magazine first recognized this category, it named just three companies to its Best Companies for Women of Color:

IBM: IBM has come up with a four-pronged strategy of recruiting, hiring, and promoting women of color:

❖ **Networking:** Women's Task Force on Multicultural Women.

❖ **Mentoring:** *La Red* (Spanish for "network"), an Hispanic networking group within IBM, offers "one-to-many" mentoring, bringing senior executives together with 50 or more women who have less than five years in the company.

❖ **Recruiting and developing women of color:** Begun at Armonk, N.Y., in 1997, the Global Women's conference draws IBM executives and managers of diverse races and ethnicities to discuss work/life challenges for women around the world. In 1998, the Multicultural Women's Symposia brought together women of color for leadership training and networking.

❖ **Outreach to girls:** IBM encourages middle-school girls to stay interested in science and math. Four years ago, IBM launched a series of technology summer camps for middle-school girls. It's sponsoring 30 camps this year.

Since 1995, the number of IBM execs who are women of color has grown from 17 to 74, with most promoted from within the company. While that represents a 335-percent boost, IBM knows it's a long way from truly tapping the talent of its minority women.

American Express: American Express (AmEx) boasts one of a handful of African-American chairmen and CEOs in the United States. That leadership has led to recruiting 19 percent of its employees from among women of color, with 2 percent of the top execs being women of color. AmEx realizes that these numbers are low so, five years ago, it began requiring a diverse slate of candidates for every job opening. Overall, the percentage of minority women in management has increased 5 percent from 2000 to 2003. The corporate culture rewards results based on a stated list of skills and attitudes required to succeed in its leadership competency model. Tapping into the flex schedules does not hamper advancement for women of color, so long as their results are stellar. This opens the door to opportunity.

Fannie Mae: Led by an African-American CEO, Franklin Raines, Fannie Mae (FM) tops the charts with its huge roster of women of color—25 percent of its workforce. In a survey of employee satisfaction, 60 percent of FM's women of color were satisfied with their advancement and 51 percent saw solid opportunities for career growth.

Fannie Mae's Assistance for Collegiate Education (ACE) allows employees at all levels to pursue a bachelor's or master's degree with full tuition reimbursement from the company. In 2002, 43 percent of the 448 participants were women of color. Job rotation, mentoring, and networking programs provide much-needed opportunities to try new skills and get the support and camaraderie necessary to be successful when going outside one's comfort zone. This ensures that the pool of qualified women of color grows so that the 16 percent of women of color managers and 9 percent of women of color executives will soon be increasing at Fannie Mae.

New Majority Rules

It is estimated that by 2008 women and minorities will make up 70 percent of workforce entrants. Eight companies are poised for this ethnographic and demographic shift according to *Working Mother* magazine: Allstate, American Express, Anthem Blue Cross and Blue Shield, General Mills, HP, IBM, JPMorgan Chase, and PriceWaterhouseCoopers. All were named to the 2005 Best Companies for Women of Color. Progressive companies institute formal mentoring and networking programs across gender and color lines; company-wide diversity training; tuition reimbursement for advanced degrees; leadership development and executive coaching; talent retention programs;

fast-track executive programs; management compensation tied to diversity initiatives; innovative recruiting strategies; internal diverse interest groups; and college internship programs.

A Prince Who Turns Out to Be a Frog

Ever date someone who was gracious, romantic, and attentive until you moved in with him? The laws of dating apply to company selection. Everyone puts their best foot forward on the first date, picking the right clothes, showering with special soap, visiting the hair salon before the big night, picking the right restaurant to make the right first impression. Companies can fool you or turn on you. Like significant others, you never know them until you've lived with them.

One such company looked great on the outside. Led by a European woman technologist, the software company that lured me was on the brink of going public. It did go public during my brief tenure, but the CEO quickly cashed out most of her stock in the first year and proceeded to drive the company into bankruptcy two years later. This woman-led company had one of the worst retention track records in the industry, with a 55 percent turnover rate per year. Compassionate she was not, often requiring lower-level workers to work 12-hour shifts in windowless computer rooms for weeks at a time.

Princes can turn into frogs, sometimes overnight. This happened at another software company, one that once boasted six women executive vice presidents, including the chief technologist. When the founders sold the company, the changes began. All six women resigned within a year. A few young women engineers and public relations experts were brought in by the new CEO to lead in key positions, but the only females in senior management were two VPs of support areas. Things actually went downhill from there. A new executive, a foreign-born CEO from a computer company known for six years of downsizing, brought in a marketing senior executive who "cleaned house." The only remaining woman executive was the vice president of human resources and a neighbor of the CEO. The prince of a company, known for its innovation, full participation, and flexible scheduling, soon became a frog, with top-down management, regular downsizing, and "an old boys' network" heading the management chain.

When Nations Bank of North Carolina bought Bank of America of California, the number of women top earners at Bank of America, once 40 percent, shrank dramatically. Kathleen Brown, former Treasurer of the State of California and responsible for the state's highest municipal bond rating at the time, left the bank soon after the merger that created a "good old boy" Southern culture of advancement, leaving little room for the progressive tenor set by the former senior executive team.

"Beauty Is as Beauty Does"

At forward-thinking companies, balancing family and work does not have to be a career-ending move.

In July of 2000, IBM created a $50 million fund for investments in work-life practices for 164 of its facilities around the world. A full 80,000 U.S. employees of IBM telecommute, saving the company $75 million in real estate. IBM practices what it preaches. It turns out that work-life balance programs are good not only for employees, but for the bottom line as well.

At Aetna Financial Services, one high-flying female executive, the CFO, Catherine Smith, spent six of her 16 years working part-time. "I've had the equivalent of five interesting jobs with increasing levels of responsibility, while running a family."

Deloitte & Touche is redefining consulting services with its formalized Work-Life Balance programs that keep consulting gigs close to home whenever possible and confine business travel to Monday through Friday for most assignments. PriceWaterhouseCoopers (PWC) hands out a *Guide to WorkLife Quality* smaller than a 3 x 5 card that employees can flip through while waiting in line to board a plane. The book actually advises employees not to take laptops, pagers, or cell phones with them on vacation. In one segment on *Supports*, PWC urges: "Invest in your friendships. Friendship doubles our joy and divides our sorrow." Under *Leisure*: "Always have a vacation planned."

The Choice Is Yours

Andrea Jung, CEO of Avon Products, has always been careful of the company she's kept. "I'm very selective in the companies I work for. I started at Bloomingdale's because it was committed to developing women. When I went to I. Magnin in San Francisco, it was to a company with a female CEO. I think it's critical that you feel you're working for a person who is committed to advancing your career. That's why I've gotten to where I am today" (*www.goldsea.com*, 1998).

Why kiss the slimy frogs when you could be kissing the handsome princes?

Diversity Pays Off

The interesting thing is that joining a women-friendly company is not just good for your career or your mental health, it's also good for your pocketbook. In a study of 353 of the *Fortune* 500, a women's research group, Catalyst, found that companies with strong women-friendly cultures perform better in the marketplace. The study divided the 353 companies into four quartiles based on representation of women in management and then compared the return on equity (ROE) and total return to shareholders (TRS). The top quartile, 88 companies with the highest gender diversity in its leadership, had a 35 percent higher ROE and a 34 percent higher TRS than the bottom quartile, 89 companies with the lowest gender diversity (*Catalyst Report*, 2004).

By choosing companies with a strong women's presence at all levels, you'll most likely be choosing a company that supports and promotes women in the workplace. More importantly, you'll be working for a financial winner that will heap rewards on you as you climb the corporate ladder. So, if you have a choice between a frog and a prince, wouldn't you rather pick a prince?

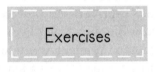

Exercises

1.   Assess your company's support of women's advancement and list the percentages:

___Percent of Top 5 Earners Who Are Women

___Percent of Women Officers—Chair, Vice-Chair, CEO, President, COO, EVP

___Percent of Women Top Executives—Director and Above

___Percent of Women Board Members

___Percent of Women Employees

___Percent of Women of Color

___Percent of Women of Color in Management

2.   Determine how serious your company is about including women in the executive suite (check all that apply, giving your company a point for each; 5 is a perfect score):

___Formal Mentoring Programs
___Formal Networking Initiatives
___Management Training
___Fast Track Programs
___Sponsorship of Women's Professional Organizations

3.   Determine if your company really does support work/life balance by checking all that apply (1 point for each check; a score of 10 or better is excellent):
___Formal Mentoring Programs?
___Flextime
___Telecommuting
___Part-Time with Benefits
___Job-Sharing
___On-Site Gym/Fitness Classes/Gym Membership Subsidy
___Compressed Workweek
___Subsidized On-Site/Near-Site Childcare
___Extended Paid Family Leave of Absence
___Job Guarantee Following Leave
___Volunteer Release Time
___Subsidized Cafeteria
___Paid 3-Week or Longer Vacation Starting the First Year
___Paid Sabbaticals
___Elder/Dependent Care Services
___Tuition Reimbursement
___On-Site University/Distance Learning
___Management Training about Flextime and Work/Life Balance
___Videoconferencing (in lieu of travel)
___Paid Childcare/Petcare for Overnight Business Travel
___Home Loan Discounts

___Employee Stock Purchase
___401(k) Company Match
___Company Vehicle
___Public Transit/Carpool Subsidies
___Relocation Benefits for All Levels

4. Does your company have a formal Mentoring Program? List three ways you could benefit from it.

5. Is there a formal Networking Initiative for Women Employees? List three steps you could take to get involved.

6. Does your company regularly sponsor women's professional organizations? Name 10 of them. Select one to attend every year.

7. Target 10 companies in your geographical area that meet the above criteria and network once a month with women employees from those companies (one way to find them is through professional organizations and via existing contacts). There really are only "six degrees of separation" (Guare, 1990); we're only six people away from meeting anyone we want to meet.

Chapter 2

"Wake up and make the cappuccino."

The Soccer Mom

There are no shortcuts to anyplace worth going.

~ Beverly Sills
American opera singer

Soccer Weekends

It's 6 a.m. on a Saturday and Kelli is up before the rest of the household. She's baking dozens of oatmeal chocolate-chip cookies for the boys on her son's soccer team. She's filling up the thermos with fresh-squeezed lemonade from the lemons in her garden. She's packing the ice chest with bottled waters. At 7 a.m., she wakes up the four boys and one girl and encourages them to get up with the aroma of banana walnut whole-grain pancakes served with Vermont maple syrup.

Kelli drives the first round of soccer teams to their Saturday morning games and stays to sell hot dogs and drinks to raise money for the team's trips. Her son, Sean, with a gash above his left eye from a missed header, runs over to her for a hug and an ice pack. Though he is 8 years old and taller than all the other boys on his team, he reluctantly accepts his mom's embrace. Kelli looks at his rapidly closing wound, bandages his forehead, and walks him over to the bench where his teammates console him.

One sales executive I'd worked for and enjoyed immensely regularly left work early Friday afternoons to attend his daughter Molly's weekend soccer tournaments, often played up and down the Eastern seaboard. I periodically touched base with him via e-mail or voicemail, but hadn't heard back from him in months. Then, out of the blue, I got this e-mail from him:

> *Dear Kathleen,*
> *Sorry I haven't been in touch. But, you know, I've gotten it all—big promotion, SVP title, stock options, IPO, multi-millions of dollars—everything I'd always wanted. You know, now that my daughter, Molly, is dead, it doesn't mean much. I'd trade it all for those soccer weekends I used to complain about.*
> *Love, Jack*

Quality Versus Quantity Time?

In the 1970s, universities conducted studies with preschoolers and uncovered a result contrary to popular thought at the time. Observing mothers and small children several hours a day over time, one university found that preschoolers felt more secure with full-time moms than with preschool care. Just knowing mom was nearby and available comforted the kids. They played more independently, with fewer behavior problems and outbursts, but with more frequent "check-ins" with their moms than children in full-time preschools. I found this out firsthand as a University of Iowa graduate preschool teacher. Kids with more "at home" time with moms versus those with full-time, long-day preschool situations came into class with fewer behavior problems and greater self-esteem, in general. Maybe that's why more college-educated American mothers are opting out of full-time work to return to full-time motherhood than at any other time in American history since the 1950s. Currently, the United States has one of the "lowest labor force participation rates for college-educated women in the developed world; only in Turkey, Ireland, Switzerland, and the Netherlands, does a smaller proportion of female college graduates work for pay" (Babcock and Laschever, 2003).

The Wake-Up Call

Amy was going through a divorce after 14 years of marriage and the only thing that got her into work every morning was the smiling face of Maria at the café, where she stopped in for cappuccino, nonfat milk, all foam. One morning, as she double-parked her Volvo, Amy knew something was dreadfully wrong. Maria wasn't smiling and her husband Pedro wasn't there. Maria didn't even look up from the steamer to say her usual bright hello. When Maria had a moment away from the onslaught of customers and went to the far side of the counter to answer a phone call, Amy asked what was wrong. A blank stare came over the pretty woman's face as Maria explained she and her husband of 15 years were getting a divorce. Amy went back to her Volvo, now tagged with a very expensive double-parking ticket; she stopped at Macy's that night after work to buy a Braun espresso machine. She realized that the $4 she was paying for cappuccinos was really paying for friendship—not a real friendship, where she knew Maria and Pedro lived upstairs from the café, that Pedro cheated on her, and that Maria never went back to school as Pedro had promised four years after they took over the café. It was a faux friendship, like the ones she had formed with her dog walker, house cleaner, gardener, handyman, personal trainer, meditation teacher, massage therapist, deli caterer, florist, baker, chiropractor, and psychologist.

Subcontracting Out Your Life?

There's only one thing as bad as doing a job you hate, and that's working so hard you wind up subcontracting out your life. If you're not careful, soon someone else will be living your life for you. The Pueblo Indians don't let you take their photograph; their tradition teaches that if you let people take your picture, they could take your soul. Yet you sign up to work longer and longer hours and don't even see how the corporation is taking your soul from you. Americans are the only citizens of the world who *give back* vacation days! This is true even though Americans average only 12 vacation days per year, far fewer than the 25 vacation days most Europeans, Australians, Canadians, and New Zealanders enjoy. Americans are giving back 421 million vacation days each year. That's an average of three vacation days per person. More than 50 percent of U.S. workers work more than 40 hours a week. In 2005, Americans were expected to give back an estimated $54 billion in vacation time (Expedia.com, 2005). What happens to the lives of these workaholics?

First, they give up cooking and grab fast food, lattés, and prepackaged meals at the market. Then, they give up walking and bicycling and drive 45 minutes or more to the office. Along with the commute, workaholics quit cleaning their houses and hire someone to do it, though they always complain that no one cleans as well or as carefully as they do. There's no time for play, so workaholics hire fitness trainers to make sure they work out. There's no energy at the end of a long day, so gardeners tend to their roses and lawns while they're away. They're not home 10 to 12 hours a day, so workaholics have to hire dog walkers to keep their puppies company and socialize them with other dogs.

Life Interrupted

Marriage eludes many highly paid, high-achieving women. Men become more attractive with success and age. Women are seen as a threat the more successful they become. Men, generally, still want to make more money than women do and be seen as the household "breadwinners." As women climb the corporate ladder, they have less and less time for finding and nurturing relationships. Working women with families still perform 90 percent of the childcare and household duties (Hochschild, 2003). Men, on the other hand, are picked up at the airport, have dinner waiting late on the table, and have children cared for by a woman who supports her husband's ambitions. Very few women have that same reception and support from men.

Many young women emulate men on the fast track to success. Only they forget one important factor in the equation: the biological clock. It doesn't tick forever and the longer you wait to become a mom, the less likely your chances. Thirty-three percent of the top 10 percent of women nationwide and 42 percent of all women in Corporate America are childless at age 40. Fertility starts to decline in the late 20s and early 30s, with an even more rapid decline around age 37 and a steep drop at age 42 (Cedars, 2003). All women are born with a finite number of eggs; as women age, the quality of the eggs declines and there's an increase of genetic abnormalities in the eggs. Women overestimate the amount of time they have on their biological clocks by five to 10 years (Hewlett, 2002).

The Backpack From Hell

At one software company, the company hands out backpacks stuffed with laptops at orientation. At first, you think, "Way cool! They really invest in their employees here." You think that until the reality sets in that the backpack is more for their convenience than yours. The reason you get this laptop is so that you can hit the ground running. The company demands 8 to 10 hours a day of meetings, so you'll need to bring the laptop home to check e-mail, develop forecasts, create strategic plans, and make PowerPoint slides that you were unable to finish while you were in all those meetings all day.

Technological Breakthrough or Breakdown?

The technological breakthroughs that have enabled 24/7 operations have led to a breakdown in family life. Universal access denies you the time with your family you used to have at home. If your boss can catch you in the car on your mobile, your commute becomes an aggravated extension of your already intense workdays. If videoconferencing can bring London, New York, and San Francisco together, your workday on the West Coast will begin at 6 a.m., not 9 a.m., and ends well past 5 p.m. Air telephones mean that even on a plane, you're never far from headquarters, making excuses for not returning voicemails instantly unusable. The blue hum of the laptop now supplants your movie time on those grueling cross-country flights. Wireless technology makes being unconnected impossible.

Instant text-messaging beeps even into your thoughts. In France, businesses shut down for two hours at lunch. The civilized practice bears witness to groups of coworkers strolling in the streets of Lyon for a *plat* at lunch and a walk to and from the restaurant. Some teachers, with lifelong appointments, walk to and from school at noon to enjoy both lunch and a refreshing nap; they consider a full-time high school teaching load to be

18 hours a week. It is no wonder "French women don't get fat." They eat a satisfying and balanced meal of natural foods at noon, followed by a walk, and get off work at five, to walk once again home. The typical 35-hour workweek leaves ample time for family, friends, exercise, and cooking healthy meals.

Is Your Life Your Own Anymore?

Have you sold your soul to the devil in the deep blue suit?

If your idea of dinner is a chicken salad from McDonald's or dinner packets from Whole Foods, maybe work is eclipsing too much of your time. If your idea of gardening is calling your gardener every week, maybe it's time to leave the office earlier to do some of your own yard work. If the only comfort you get is from your masseuse once a week, maybe it's time to pack your bags and take your beloved on a weekend surprise vacation. If the only person you reach for in crisis is a trained professional or the Employee Assistance Line, maybe it's time to make time for friends.

The Choice Is Yours

Often it is a choice. How you spend your time. How you prioritize your life. Life should not be an oxymoron when coupled with corporate and entrepreneurial success.

In fact, some of the most successful executives and business owners I've known have figured out ways to devote time to their marriages, their kids, and themselves. These folks have stood the test of time, weathered the downturns, and gone the distance. The relationships they nurture and the time they spend recharging give them the strength to withstand the rigors of corporate life.

These happy people often choose personal satisfaction over status and money. They stay in positions that afford them maximum compensation for reasonable commitment. They do jobs they love even if it means passing up promotions that would afford them greater compensation and bigger job titles. In Susan Harrow's book, *Sell Yourself without Selling Your Soul* (Harper Collins, 2002), spirituality in the workplace is the key to fulfillment. And spirituality is defined as "meaningful work." There are two components to meaningful work:

❖ Work you love.

❖ Work that helps you transcend yourself and your singular life.

To sustain the passion it takes to remain in corporate life, you need work that touches your core and connections that inspirit you (Briskin, 1996). You must, therefore, work for and with people whom you respect and for an organization with values that align with yours.

Managers and professionals who choose carefully find companies that support their needs for work/life balance. They turn down promotions that demand excessive business travel without dire consequences to their careers. They work close to home and need not move to keep their jobs or get promoted. They eschew "Platinum" status and the "Red Carpet" treatment at airports for more time with their families and friends. They consciously sometimes choose lower status positions in favor of lower stress. They occasionally make lateral rather than vertical moves in their careers to retain the benefits of continuous challenge, learning, and professional development without sacrificing health, wellness, balance, and joy.

Simply Smaller

In American culture, where bigger has always been better, it is sometimes hard to remember that bigger's price may be too dear to make the new choice truly better.

Even my mortgage broker questioned my choice of "buying down" when I went to finance my new home in a less expensive city. He was truly mystified that, mid-life, I would choose to purchase a home that cost 25 percent less than the home I left in San Francisco. He couldn't quite understand that buying a better quality of life was more important to me than clinging to my high-end San Francisco address. Putting simple living into practice, my move "down" bought me two years off to write, time to explore my new neighborhood, and time to discover new organic produce and natural foods markets, Rastafarian cafes, family-owned bookstores, multicultural churches, live music venues, dance clubs, workshops, gyms, and hiking trails. For my hyped-up, caffeine-overdosed broker answering three calls—one mobile and two landlines—at once, the thought of stepping out of the rat race was anathema. He was so successful that he lived in the highest of the high-end, on the same Tiburon peninsula where world-class tennis player Andre Agassi lived at one time, and drove the highest of the high-end sports cars. Yet, in spite of my repeated offers to get him onto the golf course at Pebble Beach, this guy with a low handicap couldn't get off the fast track long enough to take advantage of the opportunity to play one of the world's best golf courses. He confessed to never having played Pebble Beach though he loved golf and lived only three hours away from the Pacific Oceanside course. For my mortgage broker, there was never a good time to take a weekday off and play the sport he loved. Low interest rates meant more customers. High interest rates meant not enough customers. Either way, he was trading in his best years for the only adrenaline rush he got every day: the rush of closing business. There's nothing wrong with getting a rush out of closing business, but there's something seriously wrong if that's the only rush you get!

Some people laugh at my 17-year-old 240DL Volvo. "Why don't you buy a new BMW, Mercedes, or Toyota Prius?" The answer is simple. My Swedish-made fundamental car runs like new and protects me from major injury on the traffic-dense freeways and bridges of my commute to clients and universities. My Swedish mechanics keep the car in premium condition and its silver finish looks like new. The four-door car holds five people comfortably and the ample trunk carries all my gym equipment, with a special compartment even for skis. The American syndrome of buying a new car every four or five years keeps Americans in debt. Performing maintenance on a good, solidly made car is far less expensive than $500-a-month car payments that can now be diverted to weekend getaways and long-term travel plans.

From buying down to not buying at all, thinking smaller can make your life better, allowing you more time and money for the really *big* things of life.

Lighten Your Load

Clean out your closets. There is a metaphysical principle that every time you "clear out your closets" you make room for new and better things to come into your life (Ponder, 1966). Don't accumulate clothes you'll never wear or haven't worn in years. Find the nearest clothes secondhand shop for women trying to make it out of poverty. Give away your little-used suits to women who desperately need a new lease on life. It'll give you a new lease on life just knowing you've helped a single parent find a job or a homeless person get off the streets. It'll eliminate unwanted clutter from your closets and your life. It will allow you to hang on to clothes that fit well, look terrific, and lift your spirits.

One top saleswoman at Hewlett-Packard gave me this tip when I first went into sales: Buy the best. Buy a few outrageously expensive outfits that you look and feel fabulous in every time you wear them. Most of your customers will only see you once and won't remember from one infrequent meeting to the next that you wore that little Chanel number last time. They'll only remember how stunning you looked in that Vera Wang dress or hand-sewn embroidered designer jacket from Milan.

It's another way to reclaim your life. Take charge. Master your wardrobe and you master your life. Don't let an "old image" dominate the you that you have become.

Nature Nurtures

Another way to get in touch with the life you may have lost is to get out and "smell the roses." At least once a month, take a hike in a natural setting far from the blare of traffic. Take your time. Notice the scarlet pimpernel wildflowers. Hear the acorn woodpeckers and stellar jays. Touch the smooth mahogany skin of the madrone trees. Pick July blackberries. Dip your toes in a running brook and let the cold runoff from the mountains take your breath away. Roll up your pants, take off your shoes, and sink into the wet sand along the ocean, feeling the sea foam kiss your toes. Smell the eucalyptus-swept air and the crushed seeds pungent underfoot. Squeeze bay leaves in your hand and smell the river in the pale green leaves. Walk in the rain and taste the drops of water on your lips.

Take a trip to a place you've never been before. The Dalai Lama recommends going somewhere new to you at least once a year. Re-awaken your senses with bath gel from Santa Fe's Ten Thousand Waves in the Sangre de Cristo Mountains. Or, swim nude (you have to if you don't want the sea lice to nip you) in the warm, salt waters of Karaka Bay, New Zealand. Reconnect with the earth and you'll reconnect with yourself.

Make a Date with Yourself

E-mail a note to yourself. Plan ahead. Mark a day in your Palm Pilot or Blackberry. Just as you would make a date with an important client, make a date with yourself. Choose your favorite venue. It could be the Pacific Ocean at Point Reyes or the

Mountain Home on Mt. Tamalpais. It could be a desert spa in Palm Springs or Harbin Hot Springs. It could be New England in the fall or Florida in the winter. It could be as small as your own backyard or as big as an artist's retreat at Ghost Ranch in New Mexico. It could be your study or study in China.

Only you know the date that will bring you rejuvenation.

Breathe

Eastern traditions have long focused on mindfulness, which begins with the breath. The Chinese call it "chi," the Indians, "prana," the Japanese, "reiki"; it is the life force. It is your responsibility to tend to your breath, your energy center, your base of power within. Start your day with a practice of meditation, yoga, or t'ai chi to connect with this infinite source of well-being within. Daily practice gives you energy. Daily practice gives peace and harmony available regardless of circumstances. It doesn't always take a whole day to secure a daily vacation. Meditation can give you one in 20 minutes or five. So if you can't afford a day-long date with yourself, take a mini-break.

Reclaim yourself by making a date with yourself at least once a month. You wouldn't think of neglecting your staff for a month, so why neglect yourself? Reclaim your life, one small step at a time.

Put the Passion Back Into Your Life

At a couples' workshop I recently attended, participants were asked to name three things they were passionate about. Some said playing instruments; others, climbing mountains; and still others, dancing. Some named sailing, writing, hiking, gardening, sky diving, tennis, camping, cooking, quilting, or reading. Then, the facilitators asked us how often we did the things we were passionate about. Daily? Weekly? Monthly? Annually?

The facilitators made the point that "if you're not passionate in your lives, you won't be passionate in the bedroom."

One participant, a blonde, blue-eyed, 30-something telecommunications executive spoke of logging more than 200,000 frequent flyer miles to such exotic places as Hong Kong and Korea. She couldn't answer this question because, she confessed, "All I do is work." She continued, "We live in suburban hell, with a pool and a hot tub and a 3500-square-foot house that I hardly ever see!"

While I'm not suggesting you "chuck" your hard-won success, I am asking you to take a look at your life and see if it really is *your* life. If you don't have passion outside of work, you probably won't have passion in your work.

If you find you need more and more resuscitators—masseuses, trainers, psychotherapists, coaches, chiropractors, physical therapists— you may want to shift your priorities so the main person caring for you is you and not someone outside yourself.

Start small. Name one passion outside of work. Do something related to that passion every day. If you're a writer with no time to write, at least write Morning Pages (Cameron, 1992) every day. If you're a runner, get up an hour earlier and run every day. If you're a dancer with no one to dance with, take a dance class and dance once a week. If you love swimming, find a local pool with convenient hours and swim at least once a week.

The Soccer Mom Makes the Coffee

The soccer mom makes the coffee and bakes the chocolate-chip cookies for the bake sale the night before the tournament. She sews patches on the uniforms and sells hot dogs at the snack stand to raise money for the team. She chauffeurs her kids and yours. She practices kicking and head butting with the team in the backyard before tournaments. She knows the joys of victory and the agonies of defeat. She knows them because she experiences them, up close and personal. If you want more joy in your life, take a lesson from the soccer mom. Wake up and make the cappuccino before you forget how!

Exercises

1. Draw a pie chart of your current week. What percentage of your week is "hired out"? Take one segment and reclaim it. Example: You buy your lunch out every weekday. One day a week, make your lunch and take it from home. Benefits: healthier, lower-cal meals and less cost.

2. Find out what important events are coming up this month for your kids. Mark the calendar to attend at least one of your children's special events once a week this month.
    Examples:
    ❖ Soccer game
    ❖ Martial arts sparring
    ❖ Surfing competition
    ❖ Basketball tournament
    ❖ Art fair
    ❖ Piano/music recital
    ❖ Baseball game
    ❖ Debating contest

❖ Speech
❖ Theater performance
❖ Spelling bee
❖ Junior Achievement presentation
❖ Tennis tournament
❖ Swim meet

3. Cook at least one meal from scratch with in-season produce once a week during the workweek. Try a different recipe each week for 52 weeks. Benefits: (a) You'll add 52 new recipes to your repertoire; (b) you may find cooking fun again; (c) you'll be eating more nutritiously when you prepare a meal from scratch with in-season fresh vegetables and fruits.

4. With your child, make a Halloween costume this year.

5. With your family or friends, choose a Christmas, Hanukkah, or Kwanzaa theme and make your own gifts this year.
   Examples:
   ❖ Candles
   ❖ Soap
   ❖ Dry-mounted photographs
   ❖ Photo calendars
   ❖ Cookies/breads/cakes
   ❖ Woodworks
   ❖ Pottery
   ❖ Knit/crocheted/sewn objects
   ❖ Ornaments
   Make your own holiday cards this year, using one of the following media: Adobe Photoshop; digital photographs and card creation software; Roller ball etching; silkscreen; collage; or watercolor prints.

6. Reduce going out for caffe lattes or mochas to once per week. Buy an espresso machine and make your own lattes and mochas at home. Buy a stainless steel travel cup and take your coffee creations on your commute with you.

7. Eat breakfast at home every morning. Get up a half hour earlier if you must, but eat a good breakfast at home before you start your workday.

8. Try making bread at least once a year.

9. At least twice a year, host a party and make all the hors d'oeuvres for the fête.

10. Pick an activity your mom, dad, sister, or brother would like and plan to do it with them at least once a quarter if they live nearby or once a year if they are far away. One executive I know takes the entire extended family on an active vacation once a year, to a dude ranch, Club Med, High Sierra Family Camp, or University of California Bears Alumni Family Camp. If a big-time vacation is out of the question, try:

   ❖ Annual or semi-annual family reunions at someone's house
   ❖ Annual baseball game
   ❖ College football game and tailgate party
   ❖ Theater day in the city
   ❖ Free symphony/opera in the park
   ❖ Free concerts and picnics
   ❖ Annual walkathons for charity
   ❖ High tea
   ❖ Arts and crafts street fairs
   ❖ Spa
   ❖ Religious service
   ❖ Movie

11. List your passions. Next to each one, note the last time you did anything related to those passions. Pick the most neglected or most wanted and make a plan to devote time at least once a month on your long-lost passion.
    Examples:
    ❖ Hiking
    ❖ Camping
    ❖ Kayaking
    ❖ Backpacking
    ❖ Skiing
    ❖ Tennis
    ❖ Dancing
    ❖ Cycling
    ❖ Swimming
    ❖ Scuba diving
    ❖ Gardening
    ❖ Reading
    ❖ Home decorating
    ❖ Cooking

12. Keep a diary. Make an entry, even if it's only one sentence, daily. Read it every three months. See if you're spending your life the way you want to or if you are meeting someone else's expectations for you. Like budgeting, writing a diary of your actions helps you see how you're really spending your time and helps you identify areas you may want to change.

13. Plan to spend time in nature at least once a month.
    Examples:
    ❖ Walk around the lake/along the river near your home.
    ❖ Hike in a county or state or national park.
    ❖ Take off your shoes, roll up your pants, and walk along the beach.

❖   Go pumpkin hunting in a pumpkin patch.
❖   Pick berries at a berry farm.
❖   Plant a garden in your backyard.
❖   Sit out in your backyard and eat your lunch.

14.   Analyze your current work situation. If you're not doing work you love, spend some time figuring out what you love and find ways, even as a hobby, to do work you enjoy. Read or listen to Barbara Sher's *I Could Do Anything If I Only Knew What It Was: How to Discover What You Really Want and How to Get It* (Sher, 1994) or watch the PBS Special, *Creating Your Second Life After 40* (Sher, 1998).

15.   Before you buy that next house, second home, new car, or boat, list all you'll have to give up to get this new material goal. Think hard before trading in for "bigger," which may not always be "better."

16.   Clear out your closets. Donate everything you haven't worn in the last year. This leaves room in your life for clothes you really like and truly wear and eliminates clutter to make room for new and more fitting clothes.

17.   Make a date with yourself at least once a month. Mark the day on your calendar. Devote an entire day to just you. Plan it as you would any other date with someone else: pick a venue, make a reservation, and budget for the experience.
Examples:
❖   Pack a lunch and go for a hike.
❖   Bicycle beside the lake/bay/river.
❖   Attend a day-long writer's conference.
❖   Plan a trip.
❖   Take a language immersion class.
❖   Go to a spa.

❖   Play a round of golf on a weekday.
❖   Take a day-long workshop.
❖   Take a dance lesson.

Keep a log of your "dates" and, at the end of the year, identify the best ones and build in more of those the next year.

18.   List 20 things you'd like to accomplish in your lifetime that you haven't accomplished yet. Dream *big*. Don't worry if the dreams are not realistic. Remember, the secret to a happy life is to have someone to love, have something to do, and have something to look forward to. Pick one vision a year and take action toward creating that dream. For example, this is my list:

1.   Publish a book.
2.   Climb Machu Picchu.
3.   Travel down the Amazon River.
4.   Master Spanish and French.
5.   Live and work in Europe for a year.
6.   Play piano and guitar.
7.   Act in a play.
8.   Start a foundation.
9.   Travel to a different foreign country at least once a year.
10.   Live and write in New Zealand for at least four months a year.
11.   Learn to cook Asian/vegetarian cuisine.
12.   Learn to dance the tango.
13.   Write full-time.
14.   Build a kit home in the country.
15.   Learn to create digital art.
16.   Go to a week-long writer's conference each and every year.
17.   Go on a weekend spiritual retreat once a year.
18.   Play tennis in a tennis tournament every year.

19.   Camp at least once a year.
20.   Learn to sea kayak.

21.   Do a project by yourself once a year. Examples:
    ❖   Plant a garden.
    ❖   Build a table.
    ❖   Make a photo album for your relatives.
    ❖   Finish a genealogy chart.
    ❖   Make a recipe book of favorite family recipes.
    ❖   Crochet a blanket.
    ❖   Sew a quilt.
    ❖   Paint a picture.
    ❖   Paint a room.
    ❖   Write a screenplay.

Chapter 3

Trust your intuition

The Psychic

What would happen if one woman told the truth about her life? The world would split open.

~ Muriel Rukeyser
American poet

Trust Yourself

She was a top resident at Stanford University, but she came home crying almost every night. She had earned a near-perfect SAT score, was at the top of her undergraduate class at Harvard, and had finished in the top 2 percent with her MCAT scores. She was one of the best interns at Columbia Medical School. Why was she crying? A renowned surgeon, leading orthopedic rounds, basically told her, "Don't bother learning orthopedics; women aren't strong enough to set bones." The chief of surgery at Stanford sent some of the best women residents out of the surgical theater sobbing after an unfair "drubbing." The cutest interns fared the worst, with residents and chief residents alike taking advantage of them under operating tables during surgery. This Stanford resident was crying for her own demeaning experience, but, even more so, for the harassing behavior her female colleagues were subjected to every day. The story has a happy ending. This resident went on to score one of the highest rankings in the history of board certification and is now happily practicing at one of the best women's care hospitals in the country. Her perceptions kept her from sinking into self-destructive patterns on the job and her thorough preparation for all her cases kept her focused on her goal of becoming a board-certified surgeon. She never doubted her perceptions, which were confirmed in a successful class-action lawsuit launched against Stanford University Medical School for its discrimination against female medical school students, interns, residents, and surgeons. Her ability to "see through" the shenanigans of her male faculty advisers aided her in overcoming all the barriers they imposed on her to try to prevent her from joining their ranks. She trusted her intuition and it served her well.

The Personal Is the Professional

In interactions, women are better at operating from both sides of their brains: the right—holistic, intuitive, feeling side; and the left—linear, logical, verbal side. There is a scientific basis for this claim. Sophisticated brain tomography now shows that the corpus callosum, the connective tissue between the right and left hemispheres of the brain, is thicker in women than it is in men. Neurologists believe this explains woman's famed intuition and expertise in the arena of feelings.

Because women evaluate situations instantly with their intuitive powers, women are often accused of taking things "too personally." It *is* personal. Women see right through pretenses and that's a good thing.

It's not just women who operate on instinct. Entrepreneurs and visionaries often develop their philosophies of management based on "gut feelings." In fact, when asked at an elite Stanford graduate fellows' dinner for the secret of his success in founding Hewlett-Packard, Dave Packard said simply, "Hire good people and treat them well."

The Importance of Being Present

In Zulu, the greeting "Sawubona" means "I see you." It means, literally, that a person is a person because of the recognition received by others. At the very essence, everyone wishes to be seen, recognized, loved, and appreciated. It is the secret of good work relations. It is the essence of good management. Women are naturally gifted at nurturing interpersonal relations. Women live longer than men, some say, because they form and nurture lifelong friendships independent of work. One insurance study found men die, on average, within 18 months of retirement, having put all their energies into work.

"All You Need Is Love" (The Beatles, 1967)

You don't check your need for love at the door. Just because you're an adult doesn't mean you've outgrown your need to be cherished. One well-placed compliment or five minutes of attentive listening can do more to enhance work relationships and performance than all the meetings in the world. If love is your guiding principle in all your affairs, the results will be spectacular. If fear drives you, your results will falter long term.

Judgment, suspicion, criticism, and blame diminish performance. Appreciation, acceptance, attention, and approbation foster self-esteem, which translates into outstanding performance.

Women, in general, care about feelings and relationships and can use their natural gifts to make the workplace better for everyone.

What Sign Are You?

When I was the editor of an internal employee publication at Hewlett-Packard, Corporate reprimanded me for being the only HP editor to run an astrology column every month. I was also the only employee editor of the 40 or so HP divisions whose employees raced to pick up the employee newsletter when it came out every month. The column everyone turned to? Astrology, of course.

While not politically correct, I *knew* my readership of 490 employees working in an integrated circuits manufacturing facility 24 hours a day, five or six days a week. Even the R&D engineers, who pretended to view astrology as fluff, turned to the astrology column before any other technical article. Dale Carnegie, years ago, found that the secret to "winning friends and influencing people" was to encourage people to talk about their most favorite subject—themselves—and to say, often, the word they most loved to hear—their name. By writing horoscopes, I spoke to that need—employees had to find out more "about themselves."

The Luv 'Em Strategy

Herbert Kelleher, former CEO of Southwest Airlines, unabashedly touted his business philosophy in *Fortune* magazine as the "luv everyone" religion behind Southwest's meteoric rise from a commuter flight company in Texas to the third-largest airline in the United States. Despite the risk of harassment lawsuits, orange and brown shorts-clad employees of Southwest hug everyone from employees to customers. It is almost as if they take the adage "three hugs a day for minimum mental health" seriously. Their approach netted high customer satisfaction ratings and drove up sales. In today's tough travel business, Southwest is one of the only airlines in the black. The first airline to wear shorts sticks to its mission: 30 years of low fares. It's printed on the cocktail napkins. It's posted on the Website. It goes to the heart of every frequent flyer's itinerary planning: Where can I get the cheapest flight? It's a very personal and straightforward message from a very personal airline. The personal is the professional. Southwest Airlines built a business on this principle.

Count the Cost

Some management gurus would call this philosophy "soft" and outdated. However, you never outgrow your need for love. You don't leave companies; you leave managers. Most often, a positive relationship with one's immediate supervisor is the number one predictor of employee satisfaction. Beloved employees make loyal employees. Loyal employees reduce the costs associated with recruiting, hiring, and training new employees. Some recruiting experts estimate that the cost of replacing a professional employee is $25,000, while replacing a CEO can ring up as much as $1 million in out-of-pocket recruiting and sign-on bonus expenses.

The Unholy Split

"Keep a stiff upper lip." "Never let them see you sweat." "Keep your personal life separate from your professional life."
You've heard such advice. It usually came from the football coach, drill sergeant, or boss. It's used to keep you in line. Many of you try to do it. When you walk into the front lobby of your company, you check your heart at the door.

First, it is physically impossible to cut off your emotions this way. Second, it is actually damaging to your health to attempt to mask all your feelings. To deny an integral part of you at work cuts you off from your power source.

One law firm in San Francisco actually takes lawyers off big cases for a full year following a divorce filing. They realize that no matter how professional or expert an attorney may be, going through personal turmoil undermines his or her effectiveness. This kindness is returned a hundredfold when the divorced attorney returns to full performance a year later. Now, the firm has some of the most loyal and dedicated employees on staff.

American Gothic (Chicago Art Institute, 1930)

The Calvinistic notion of hard work permeates American culture. The Protestant work ethic inspired Grant Wood's *American Gothic,* a painting of an unsmiling Iowa farm couple. If it's fun, it can't be work. And if it's work, it can't be fun. In fact, many managers are so fearful of fun that if they "catch" employees having fun, they feel they've caught them doing something wrong.

Paradoxically, the opposite is true. High-performing companies create a fun-filled atmosphere where creativity and entrepreneurial spirit flourish. CoreStates breaks for story time with the preschoolers of parent employees located in the playground adjacent to its main lobby in downtown Philadelphia. Washington Mutual sponsors charity golf tournaments and sends its top mortgage loan brokers to play.

Share Your Feelings

Most managers adhere to the philosophy that you should "keep a tight lid" on what you share with your employees.

Contrary to the common wisdom, the best managers I've ever had shared their feelings with me. I became one of those managers.

When I was going through a painful breakup, I told my staff and colleagues. I had been trained not to share these deep feelings, but they were so overwhelming at the time that I couldn't hide them. To my surprise, staff brought me flowers. Colleagues took me to lunch and to the gym. Managers looked the other way when I hid in my office. I survived five layoffs at this company during one of the most trying times of my life. I'm sure that sharing my feelings, building and nurturing positive relationships, along with solid prior performance, contributed to my being spared.

Get to Know Your Staff on a Personal Level

The best management technique I've found came from one of my staff. When scheduling quarterly off-site team-building activities, one staff member suggested that every staff person plan one of the quarterly meetings. While it was hard for me to relinquish the control for staff development, I agreed, thereby encouraging more loyalty and performance than all my admonishing or didactic one-on-one coaching sessions.

This same staff member took us all to a flight simulator game facility in Mountain View, where I discovered that her father had been a World War II pilot. Another member took us to an old-fashioned ice cream parlor in Oakland. She brought her two children and husband along and I learned more about what motivated her in that one off-site meeting than in nine months of working together. I discovered that her husband was a musician and stay-at-home father, and that she was performing Herculean feats to get into the office every day by 9 a.m.

One Big Happy Family

While many of you may be skeptical of corporate team-building exercises that force you to belong to a high-performance team, true team spirit can bring a joy to the workplace you may have yet to experience. Because women are the mothers in the culture, they naturally know how to create a family feeling, in the best sense, at work.

One woman manager achieved this sense with her team-building activity involving both her and her preteen son. The two of them baked dozens of sugar and gingerbread cookies and brought them into work for a staff meeting held during December. Armed with multi-colored frostings and holiday decorations, this single parent hosted one of the most creative, lively, and cheerful team-building activities in company history. The low-cost activity, cookie decorating, involved everyone. Vice presidents in pin-striped suits stepped into the room, loosened their ties, and laughed like children as they ate the pink-frosted head off the gingerbread man and pressed red hots into buttons on the gingerbread man's chest. Button-down women executives smiled broadly as they sprinkled multicolored nonpareils into the green- and pink-frosted Christmas tree cookies. The activity, which was not a contest, brought out the spirit of play and easy camaraderie.

In play, people reveal who they are. In play, people find their true selves and the true selves of others. This discovery is the basis for real team-building. You recognize the "good spirit" in the other and, though aware of differences and conflicts, focus on the soul of another, which, at core, is the same as your own. If you can engender this kind of environment, you really can create an "all for one, one for all" mentality in your department, your division, or your company.

Focus on the Similarities, Not on the Differences

If you want to know the secret to right relations, focus on how you are the same as, not on how you are different from, your colleagues. Only by revealing your personal likes and dislikes, hobbies, and pastimes can your colleagues get to know you and begin to trust you as a member of the team.

Everyone in today's corporate environment is adept at sending e-mails, finding information on the Internet, and creating spreadsheets. That level of commonality rings hollow. It doesn't touch the deeper side of people, the place where spirit resides. Instead of *USA Today*-style sound bites, attempt to have real conversations and inject real messages into your "corporate communications." Sharing some personal anecdote or witty observation in a standard e-mail will not only help form the bonds needed for true teamwork, but it will also make your colleagues stand up and take notice. One executive said he always read my e-mails because they were short, fascinating, and often witty. They were, by no means, standard. Sharing your humanity in an e-mail strengthens the bonds that help you withstand the winds of economic challenges and market forces.

This was very evident in the great slowdown in profits during the mid-1980s at Hewlett-Packard. All managers were asked to take 10 percent pay cuts while maintaining a full-time work schedule. Staff members were asked to take 5 percent cuts and every other Friday off until, six months later, 15 percent profit levels returned.

The personal connection established within the creative arts team was so tight that not one deadline slipped, nor was one budget overextended during the slowdown. Off-site in-service training sessions continued to fuel the motivational flame of the team, although these were held in managers' homes with potluck meals instead of in hotels with outside facilitators and catered lunches. Within two years, that HP sector owned the printer market, which it continues to dominate to this day.

Personal Best

The "100 Best Companies to Work for in America" have this in common: Employees feel valued, listened to, empowered, and honored for their unique contributions. Regularly, Milton Moskowitz and Robert Levering rank the best companies in America based on an in-depth analysis of company culture and publish the results in *Fortune* magazine. In a study of 1,000 large and mid-sized firms, these 100 are selected for their financial success, a success that comes largely from developing and sustaining a culture where people are cherished.

Successful companies allow a broad range of personal freedom. Personal expression in dress, jewelry, haircuts, communication, and is a hallmark of the firms chosen. REI so heavily discounts its clothing that employees want to wear the recreational retailer's clothes. At Sun Microsystems, employees show up in everything from shorts to suits and, for those telecommuting, sweats! And the boss, Scott McNealy, plays ice hockey with the troops and has since the company started more than 14 years ago. Charles Schwab shares the profits; more than 84 percent of employees feel they get their fair share at Schwab. Deloitte & Touche understands the need for personal time and has a program to limit weekend travel for all its consultants—men and women, single and married alike—hence, its leadership role in work/life balance. At American Skandia, take-home meals and at-work grocery delivery, daycare, and hair salons demonstrate the insurance company's awareness that when employees' personal needs are met, they do their best work. At Amgen, 95 percent of employees say they're proud of what the biotech firm accomplishes. This is in concert with an on-site childcare center and a weekly farmers' market. Genentech, voted the number one best company to work for in America by Moskowitz and Levering, grants sabbaticals, celebrates with weekly beer bust "ho-ho's," and allows scientists and engineers to pursue pet projects for 20 percent of their workweeks. Every year, scientists defend requests for research dollars in a Research Review staffed by 13 Ph.D.'s. Fully 90 percent of new development never goes to market—a stunning commitment to creativity in an industry where it takes an average $800 million and 12 years to develop new drugs (*Fortune*, January 20, 2006). The human element is attended to at all these top 100 companies. No effort is made to downplay the personal lives of its employees; in fact, the personal needs of employees are brought to the forefront and addressed head on. It's no surprise that the top 100 companies are among the top-performing companies in the Fortune 500.

Personal best translates to company best.

TMI

There is a caveat, however. When does personal revelation constitute the teenager's lament, "Too much information!" which is often thrown at parents when they start sharing bedroom life details or personal hygiene habits with their offspring? There is a danger, obviously, in revealing the personal in a professional environment. One businesswoman confesses she's a recovering alcoholic with 12 days of sobriety and everyone's watching and waiting for her to "fall off the wagon" at the annual sales kick-off. One brings her anti-depressant prescription bottles to work and shows her manager, who is now attributing her tardiness to depression. Still another reveals he likes to go to parties with his college friends and engage in illegal recreational drug use. Why does anyone need to know this in a work environment?

When is personal information too much information to share? Well, one rule of thumb is that if you don't want the information posted on the company bulletin board outside the cafeteria, don't tell anyone at work.

Communication is an art, not a science. Deciding what and with whom to share your personal life at work is a judgment call. Areas that build bridges include sharing family stories, hobbies, interests, books read and movies seen, sports enjoyed, theater and civic events attended, and charities supported.

It is a fine line between revelation and exhibitionism. Revelation provokes greater understanding and closeness. Exhibitionism attracts voyeurs. Voyeur-based interest is laden with judgment, derision, gossip, and mean-spirited intent.

If you do not want to expose yourself to the prurient interests of your colleagues, don't share with them aspects of yourself that are sacred and meant only for a select few in your personal life.

Sharing Does Not Mean Tell All

There is a misconception in this generation that leads to unnatural, premature, and unwelcome sharing. You meet someone for the first time and the person tells you at dinner that he's just had a colonoscopy. You're on a plane and your seatmate tells the story of his painful divorce during the entire flight from California to New York. A new staff member joins the group and tells everyone at the department meeting how lonely she is since she moved to this new city.

Rather than elicit the support you may so desperately need, inappropriate sharing turns people off. You become a pariah to be avoided. By answering an innocuous, "How are you?" with the story of your painful breakup, your work colleague will probably never ask you that question again. As in any relationship, revelation is built on trust. And trust is built on both affinity and time. If you feel depressed, get professional help. Tell those feelings to a therapist or support group. Save those revelations for an appropriate venue, not for work.

At a basic level, work is about survival. The Darwinian principle of "survival of the fittest" operates at work whether you like it or not. So in the workplace, you do need to protect yourself. You need to ensure your own survival first.

You can say you're scared about an impending reorganization without going into your early childhood foster care and maternal abandonment as an explanation of why change is so traumatic for you. You can say you're disappointed in a 4 percent raise without telling your supervisor about all the disappointments of your father's lack of interest in your school achievements. You can say you're hurt by the public criticism of your award-winning brochure without telling your boss how your fifth-grade teacher humiliated you for not pronouncing "Buchanan" correctly.

You and only you determine what is appropriate for you to share. Trust your intuition. You're good at it.

Personally, It's Good Business

Hewlett-Packard was ahead of its time. The company that started in 1939 believed in management by objectives because it trusted that every employee wanted to do a good job. It believed that employees didn't need to be micromanaged and told how to do specific tasks, but only needed to be given the goals; the path to those goals was left to them. Employees all wear name tags because HP knows what Dale Carnegie has always taught: "Remember that a person's name is to that person the sweetest and most important sound in any language." Formal dress, executive parking spaces, and palatial office suites all gave way to informal dress, undesignated parking for all employees, and casual, open partitions in lieu of offices. I was surprised the day I went to HP's corporate offices on Page Mill Road to get the CEO's written approval on an important customer document to find the CEO, in a modest partition, a little bigger than mine, working on piles of paperwork. This, more than any corporate values speech, spoke to me as a frontline HP employee of the exemplification of equality and fairness.

Excellent companies amplify employee differences rather than bury them, the way the old IBM dark suit, white shirt, and red tie did. Tandem Computers offers only one rule of dress when in training for sales: Always dress as well as your customer. That, rather than a long list of specific colors and cuts, made sense. A global economy demands this respect for a wide variety of cultures and norms. Differentiation is an asset in a global economy.

Please and Thank You

You learned it in preschool, but how often do you forget in the heat of deadlines to say please, and when the crisis is over to say thank you?

When asked the secret of his success, one multimillionaire in Texas said, "You wouldn't believe me if I told you."

"No, really. I'd like to know," I said.

"Well, it's so simple; you wouldn't do it even if I told you," he replied.

"No, tell me. I really want to know."

"Well, okay. Here it is: Write three handwritten thank-you notes a day, every day."

A Real Partner

My personal relationship with a German vice president of an e-commerce software company contributed to the biggest e-commerce deal in my company's history. That relationship forged joint marketing efforts at trade shows, media interviews, and joint Web-marketing programs. This company went on to become the highest IPO in the history of the German stock exchange. Our personal relationship, nurtured with notes and lunches, enabled me to identify obstacles and remove barriers to our mutual success.

Customers Are People, Too

When selling to bank senior executives on the East Coast, I always brought a *See's* chocolate bar for them in my briefcase. This token gift from San Francisco almost always brought a smile to the most corporate gray suits in Manhattan and Boston. I always followed meetings with a thank-you premium from our company and a personal note. This elicited previously unheard-of customer testimonials despite corporate policies against endorsements. Many people forget that customers are people first, with the same needs and wants. As a woman, the personal touch comes naturally and is expected in the cultural norms, so you can easily use it to your advantage.

Everyone knows it costs more to get a customer than to keep one. Operations that improve customer loyalty 5 percent improve profits 25 to 85 percent (Harvard University, 1995).

Personally Speaking

As a woman, you've always known how to follow your inklings. You know your greatest skill is in your ability to "read" the underlying emotions of any business situation. Rather than run from it, embrace your natural tendency to trust your instincts about the personal dynamics affecting the business relationships. Forget all those rules they taught you about hiding your real self. In the personal is the power to inspire, motivate, and change the world. Honoring the psychic in you is where your real power lies. Trust your intuition. You can bank on it.

Exercises

1. Write at least one handwritten thank-you note a week, every week, for 52 weeks. At the end of the year, track any successes that may have been the direct result of those actions.

2. Take your staff off-site at least once a month and (with their permission) only allow "personal," non-shop-talk, conversations.

3. Designate a rotating member of your staff to plan one team-building off-site meeting at least once a quarter.

4. Take each of your staff out to lunch at least once a quarter and uncover personal interests, hobbies, community involvement, or home pressures during those lunches.

5. Play board games, such as Monopoly, Trivial Pursuit, Pictionary, Scrabble, or even Charades. These are games that enable you to get to know one another better at one large off-site per year.

6. Find the positives in your staff, colleagues, and managers, and focus your conversations on those positives. Do this daily. Record the results in a diary of "positives." Remember, what you focus on grows.

7. Share your feelings with your staff and team members. Use "I" messages when sharing feelings. Limit your confrontations to just the issue at hand. Don't bring a litany of complaints into the negotiation of a conflict.

8. Tell some, not all. Select the information you feel comfortable sharing, then share liberally. In your office

or cubicle, put up photos, quotations, calendars, posters, or other items that reflect your personal style. Ask personal questions about the partner/spouse, kids, pets, house, hobbies, sports, and community activities of your staff, colleagues, managers, and others.

9. Find areas of personal interest that you have in common with your colleagues and forge new bonds in those areas:
   ❖ Play a round of golf together.
   ❖ Play a set of tennis at your club.
   ❖ Spend a day sailing together.
   ❖ Attend a play, symphony, or opera together.
   ❖ Visit an art exhibit together.
   ❖ Go to a reading at a local bookstore.
   ❖ Take a class together.
   ❖ Work out at the company gym together.

10. Become a family-friendly manager. Adjust schedules and incorporate flextime to accommodate busy parents and harried partners. Support telecommuting where feasible. Bring kids to work and let staff bring their kids to work when there are childcare issues at home.

11. Host off-sites that are activity based and involve everyone:
   Examples:
   ❖ Billiards
   ❖ Beach volleyball
   ❖ Softball
   ❖ Board games
   ❖ Charades

10. Become a family-friendly manager. Adjust schedules and incorporate flextime to accommodate busy parents and harried partners. Support telecommuting where feasible. Bring kids to work and let staff bring their kids to work when there are childcare issues at home.

12.   Create a "no dress code" environment where staff, when not in front of customers, partners, or new recruits, can wear whatever individually expresses who they are.

13.   Host frequent informal gatherings of the entire staff:
   ❖   Brown-bag lunches
   ❖   Wine/cheese parties
   ❖   Beer busts
   ❖   Potlucks
   ❖   Movie matinee off-sites
   ❖   Company-sponsored charity events, such as AIDS walkathons, and Girl Scout Cookie sales
   ❖   Call customers on a regular basis just to converse. Five minutes a week, once a month may be all you need to be in contact. Lunch once a quarter can enhance long-term relationships.

14.   Invite customers, colleagues, and partners to speak at your company, your class, your community board, or your child's school.

15.   Invite customers to sit on your board of directors, advisory board, customer executive round table, or users' groups.

16.   Send out a brief, personal e-news blurb once a month to friends, colleagues, staff, customers, and partners just to stay in touch.

17.   Bring or regularly send small tokens of your appreciation to staff, managers, customers, and partners:
   ❖   Birthday cards/presents
   ❖   Production intro giveaways
   ❖   Holidays at least once a year. (New Year's is better than Christmas or Hanukkah and is more memorable.)

Chapter 4

Party your way to the top.

The Socialite

*Each friend represents a world in us, a world
possibly not born until they arrive, and it is only
by this meeting that a new world is born.*

~ Anaïs Nin
French writer

This Southern Belle learned early the difference between crinoline and taffeta. She learned that four things can make any party festive: candles, fresh flowers, balloons, and themes.

California Governor Schwarzenegger offered her a job. The Mayor of San Francisco wouldn't let his favorite party planner extraordinaire go. From the symphony's Black and White Ball to Dianne Feinstein's wedding with 7,000 guests, Charlotte Maillard Schultz knows how to throw a party. She's festooned San Francisco with red and gold balloons for 49er Super Bowl wins and lit up the Golden Gate Bridge for a 50th Anniversary

Walk that sagged the span when 800,000 people trekked across the suspension bridge.

Charlotte Maillard Schultz knows all the right people, from her husband, former Secretary of State George Schultz, to the Gettys, to Prince Charles and Camilla, and to her sidekick of 20 years, Stanlee Gatti. The Art Commissioner and she have "left their hearts"—multicolored, mixed-media sculptures—all over the city. The socialite who organized one of the biggest inaugural bashes in city history has a staircase in City Hall named after her. She turned up at the 30th anniversary party of Beach Blanket Babylon in a Wonder Woman costume. Even at age 70, Ms. Schultz can turn heads! At a surprise thank-you party for 40 years of service as San Francisco's Chief of Protocol, the ever-diplomatic Schultz said, "This has not been a job; I'm not sure I should be thanked for something that was a privilege. I wake up in the morning and see this great city and I say if I don't pay my dues, they may send me back to Texas!"

The Network *Is* the Job

At the age of 60, with the sun-drenched skin of a tennis coach, she managed to get a job in the worst recession in California history. Not just any job. A great job. She was a mother and a grandmother. Laid off from a golf academy at a prestigious golf course, she suffered all the anxiety of the economic times, along with the added stress of being older than just about every other applicant. She had not worked in the financial industry for four years. She had been running the sales operations of a golf school. It was not her track record of selling golf packages, nor her earlier wholesale banking experience, that got this seasoned manager her next big job. It was her socializing with the senior vice president of the bank she targeted as her next employer. It was the three or four golf rounds she played with the woman executive when she went to Southern California to visit her sister. It was the occasional dinner when she was in town. It was the friendly e-mails and quick phone calls just to say hello. In short, it was the network and not the job experience that secured her the position heading up the San Francisco Bay Area office. Though she thought she'd lose the offer as soon as human resources checked her driver's license and uncovered her age, she not only landed the executive management position, but also built up a lagging operation so successfully that she had to open a second office in less than a year.

How does she recruit new staff? By taking them out to play a round of golf. How does she motivate staff? By taking them out to SBC Ballpark to watch the San Francisco Giants play. She knows how to "Party Like It's 1999" (Prince, 1982) and that ability to have fun socializing led her to double her staff and revenues the first year on the job.

Party Hearty

I don't go to parties to meet business contacts. I love parties. Not only that, but I have managed to write off nearly every party I've thrown in the past 10 years. At one, a 1940s theme prevailed, with guests in period costumes, learning to dance a basic East Coast Swing. By the end of the rotating-partners and instructor-led dance lesson, a friend referred me to his company to consult with him on a strategic marketing plan. It's not just my parties, but all parties that offer an opportunity to schmooze. As with everything, the best schmooze is one in which you delight in the person and the conversation just for the sake of the interaction, with no intent to cut a business deal. Because I love talking to a variety of people, parties offer a terrific avenue for meeting and greeting new folks.

Last month, I went to a graduation party of a young MBA student who considered me a mentor. Her best friend was there and it turned out that her friend's lifelong dream was to complete her college degree. As a representative of a small, private university in the Oakland Hills, I was in a position to help this

African-American woman fulfill her deepest desires. By the fall, she will be enrolled in a pre-law humanities degree program for working adults.

This month, at a summer pool party, I was playing water volleyball with a former athlete. When we got out of the pool, she asked me what I did for a living. When I told her I was a writer, she offered to sponsor a reading of my work at her newly opened wine-tasting cyber bar near the Convention Center in San Francisco.

Paradox

The trick to networking at a party is not to network at all. The less compelled you feel, the more people will be drawn to you naturally. It is almost a zen practice. To be in the moment. When you meet new people, focus on your moment with them. There is nothing more flattering than the full attention of another person.

Often, a social contact made today may not materialize into a business relationship for many years. It doesn't matter. The social relationship has value in and of itself.

Network for Network's Sake

You've all heard about networking. You've all taken workshops or attended professional women's lunches where the primary purpose was to network. It's important to realize that trying to network, opportunistically, often backfires. However, enjoying the process of meeting and greeting, nurturing relationships, and building friendships attracts the people you need to succeed. Women are natural socialites, learning from a very young age how to host parties with miniature tea sets and invited friends.

If you put as much or more energy into building your network as you do into learning the technical aspects of your job, you will succeed beyond your wildest dreams.

The Glass Ceiling Report (1995) identified the lack of networking as one of the main barriers to women's advancement.

Your EQ Is More Important Than Your IQ

Emotional intelligence (EQ) (Goleman, 1995) refers to the capacity for being self-aware, harnessing emotions productively, reading feelings, handling relationships with interpersonal sensitivity, building bonds, feeling empathy, exhibiting flexibility, and demonstrating resilience. These social and emotional skills are more important in flattened, non-hierarchical, collaborative organizations and critical in a global economy.

In fact, a 40-year longitudinal study of 80 Ph.D. UC–Berkeley scientists found that those scientists with high emotional intelligence—the ability to socialize, empathize, and relate, among others—achieved four times the success of their equally qualified counterparts. At AT&T, IBM, and PepsiCo, the top sales performers (with superior people skills) brought in $6.7 million in sales per person, more than twice the average. In studies of competency models for 181 positions in 121 large companies, emotional competencies were found to be twice as important as intellect and expertise (*www.e.i.haygroup.com*).

Women naturally excel in the EQ arena. Girls, from a very young age, are trained to be sensitive to the feelings of others and to "read" situations from an emotional standpoint.

While the Boys Play, the Girls Slave Away

Early on, boys learn to play. They never stop. First, Little League. Then, soccer and snowboarding. Then, on to high school and college intercollegiate and intramural sports. Just because men leave the locker rooms behind when they put on the gray suits in the corporate corridors doesn't mean they leave play behind.

Men continue to play. They join company softball and basketball leagues. They run marathons and 10K races. They bicycle. They purchase box seats at the baseball park, ostensibly for customers, and go to baseball games in the middle of the workday! As they advance, they play golf, golf, and more golf.

Is it any wonder that more deals are cut on the golf course than anywhere else? More than 90 percent of the top Fortune 500 executives are golfers (Woo, 2002). One boss bragged about his Friday rounds with clients. He showed no remorse at being in the Hamptons every Friday afternoon playing golf.

Women, by contrast, feel guilty about taking "time off work to play." As with networking, women don't realize that playing is an integral part of building relationships. Take a page from the boys. Go out for drinks. Play a round of golf on a Friday afternoon. Take your customers and staff out to a ball game on a weekday. One of the best bonds I ever built was with a sales rep when we went to a Broadway play the night before an important customer meeting in New York. I learned more about him in one evening than I had known in a year of working together. We secured the deal with ease the next day.

Until women account executives and business managers learn to take "company time" to play, they'll never master the principles of networking. They'll never leverage the relationships that could catapult their careers far more than late hours in front of the computer screen.

Women will have to battle stereotypes. More difficult yet, you'll have to stop the voice in your head that says, "Work hard." You'll have to put a stop to the guilty mantra that repeats, "You're not really working. You're just goofing off. You don't have time for this."

Women executives make time for hairdressers and manicurists. But how many deals are cut in beauty salons?

"Develop a Good, Strong Play Ethic" (Citicorp, 2004)

It's more than just going out and hitting a bucket of balls with a customer; it's incorporating the spirit of play at work. Play rejuvenates. Play inspires. Play motivates. Ultimately, play makes a connection between body and mind and between people.

Now, finally, women have their own Bohemian Grove, that 130-year-old encampment of 2,700 of America's male elite. The men gather in the redwoods of Northern California for two weeks every year to dress up in women's clothes and stage plays, to play instruments, to hike, play tennis, and have fun. Counting George W. Bush, A.W. Clausen, Thomas Watson, Jr., Joseph Coors, Clint Eastwood, and Henry Kissinger among its ranks, this club is more than fun. It offers such an attractive network that there is a waiting list of 3,000 to join and it takes, usually, 15 to 20 years on that list and two member referrals before a man gets into the 99 percent all-white, all-male club. Now, an invitation-only meeting of the top 29 women in business, government, and academe, meet to network and play at the Belizean Grove (*Business Week*, 2001).

Networking Is More Strategic Than Working

The biggest mistake women make is working too small. Mistaking performance for results, women often concentrate too intensely on the tactical and forget the strategic. They emphasize the details and miss the overall patterns. They focus on the work and forget the process. Working late into the night is not the road to success. More education, training, and longer hours will advance you less than building your network both inside and outside the organization.

Extend the Network

Once you've realized that the most important career move you'll ever make is to develop and nurture your network, begin to expand it. One sure way to extend your network is to stay in touch with colleagues, employees, and managers once they've left the company. Many women make the mistake of socializing internally only and miss opportunities to expand their networks in this very simple way. More than one colleague I've kept in touch with on a personal level has led to a new job or a new consulting contract. That's not why I've kept in touch, but it has proven a useful tool for maintaining and extending my network.

How Do You Network?

In the flurry of daily demands, it's easy to neglect this vital aspect of your career development. It's natural to rest on the laurels of your accomplishments in a comfortable job situation. But, as any bear market will show you, no job is truly secure. Even the most productive companies—Intel, IBM, Nortel, Cisco, Nations Bank, Merrill-Lynch, Charles Schwab, GE—can fall on hard times. Even the most secure jobs—U.S. government, city and state governments, universities—can become insecure in a cost-cutting time following a major election, reorganization, technology shift, drop in enrollment, revenue shortfall, or tax law change.

Networking is like fitness and health regimens that you must do regularly to prevent major setbacks and injuries. You must do them when you're healthy; you shouldn't wait until you're recovering from a major illness to embark upon a regime.

Like any good regimen, you will form a habit only after a full eight weeks (Weil, 1997) of practicing the new behavior.

How can I possibly network daily, you ask? Well, your network can take the form of a five-minute e-mail to a colleague who's left the company or to a current customer. You can take a few minutes to call an old boss or spend three minutes at the company water cooler to chat with someone from another department.

Interspersed with these small, daily opportunities to network, make room in your schedule for the bigger moments, such as a lunch off-site once a week, a professional meeting once a month, a board meeting once a quarter, and a conference once a year.

Boards Keep You From Getting Bored

If you're tired of hearing about business and it's what you do all day, join a community board of directors. Most churches, nonprofit agencies, colleges, and schools are desperate for volunteer board members.

As with anything you do, follow your interests. If you want to see girls blossom, become a Girl Scout leader. If you want to help underprivileged kids, become a mentor. If you like sports, coach a team. If you want spiritual community, join your church's lay ministry council or your temple's planning committee. If you love writing, join a writer's group. If you love gardening, beautify your neighborhood by planting trees with your neighbors. If you want to improve schools, volunteer. If you want to make a difference, raise funds for your favorite charity.

Think Globally, Act Locally

One of the best ways to broaden your network is to travel. Not only will you meet people from other states, regions, countries and cultures, but you'll also add to your social skills. The surest way to achieve "right relations" is to uncover areas of common experience and common interest and focus on those in conversations and joint activities. The burgeoning of soccer in the U.S. has led Americans to the international language of sport that extends beyond the "football" field.

Foreigners like nothing better than to hear a complimentary conversation about their native country when visiting America. Regional differences exist throughout America and people from Michigan to New York like hearing good things about their home states when far from home. Consider these examples of conversation openers:

> "Downtown Detroit's People Mover transit system let me right off in Greek town. I went into religious arts stores to purchase lapis 'worry beads' for $5 and into a Greek restaurant for my first taste of souvlaki."

> "Who would think that one of the best places to meet New Yorkers is under the Brooklyn Bridge in the DUMBO Arts District? We sipped hand-squeezed lemonade at the DUMBO General Store during the dog days of August. There, we met a jazz musician and a Puerto Rican lesbian couple. Then, we took a walk around a stone sculpture outdoor park and talked to the artists who had made the public art. DUMBO will forever remain New York for me."

> "When I was in Rotorua, New Zealand, that advanced luge was fast. We had a blast careening down the concrete paths, going airborne over the bumps, and sailing off the turns!"

> "The Picasso Museum in the Rue de Roziers district of Paris was buzzing on a Sunday. In fact, the Jewish neighborhood was the only 'happening' place in the Catholic city that effectively shuts down on Sundays."

> "The Sergio Bustamante studio in Mexico housed some of the sculptor's best work. The jewelry

pieces were truly art and the prices were unbelievable. It was worth the cab ride from Guadalajara to see the artists in their studios in this little community of painters, sculptors, and potters."

"Whistler Mountain on New Year's Eve as seen from the cross-country ski paths could not have been more spectacular. A year after the ski lift accident, the ski patrol skied down the two mountains with lit torches, the only red lights against the white mountains in the black night three hours north of Vancouver, Canada."

Saying something positive about the home country or state of your guest is an excellent way to bridge the gap between cultures.

Learning another language can give you a window into other cultures. For example, why are there so many tones in Chinese and more than 100 Kanji characters? Why is Arabic read right to left? Why are Greek characters different from English language ones? Why are parts of speech designated as feminine or masculine in the Romance languages? In Spanish, why is there a formal *usted* and a familiar *tu?* What is the meaning of the extensive use of the imperfect tense in French and the subjunctive tense in Spanish? How do these nuances of language reveal nuances of culture?

Long before I taught solution selling techniques in Paris, I learned French in a dusty room at a wooden desk on a wrought iron runner on the second floor of St. Paul's High School in San Francisco. Sister Mary Immaculae made us conjugate verbs by writing all six forms of the most popular verbs over and over again. That's how I knew how to soften my approach to the French by using the imperfect tense in that Issy les Molineux office building those damp days in Paris.

The days of picking "cots" in San Jose and jiving with the Mexican girls in Spanish prepared me for training account executives in Miami who came from all over Latin America for class. One video clip from the Chairman of Compania de Telecomunicaciones de Chile was saved from the clipping floor by some clever translating and editing in Spanish learned in "la communidad."

Networking Is the Thing Itself

The best networking of all is the networking done naturally. By following your natural affinities, you will connect with people you enjoy and enrich your present life with the rich diversity of your associations. By not limiting your network to obviously self-serving activities, you will enjoy a broad support system that can help you find the best doctors in town, the best realtors, a good financial planner, an expert lawyer, good schools, a new job, a better investment, honest mechanics and, even, possibly, your lifelong partner or spouse.

My grandmother was the greatest example of this. When I was a young girl, she took me with her everywhere in San Francisco. She took me to the Little Sisters of the Poor convalescent home to visit her friends who were ill or disabled. She took me to funeral masses and wakes and then out to dinner downtown. She took me to hotels to meet her "old lady friends" who gave me the rice pudding and fried chicken they couldn't eat. One emblematic day, she took me to a church dinner at St. Paul's to benefit the deaf community. She sat at a table among men and women furiously signing while she ate her canned peas and roast beef. I asked her, "Gram, you're not deaf. You don't use sign language. What are you doing here?" She smiled and nodded and gestured to her non-hearing friends. "I'm here to support them. I don't have to be deaf to communicate!" It was a wonderful object lesson in finding the common ground in the most uncommon of circumstances.

Get Out of the Office

Get out of the office and into the world. Work for companies that support your involvement in your community. Schwab's former co-CEO, David Pottruck, has served Thanksgiving Dinner to homeless people at Glide Memorial Methodist Church in the Tenderloin District of San Francisco every year for the past 11 years. Hewlett-Packard has lent executives to trade schools in Silicon Valley and given minority managers release time to help underrepresented minority students in the Math, Engineering, and Science Achievement (MESA) programs.

What If I Don't Have Time?

If you're a single mom or a full-time student, working full-time, you probably don't have as much time as your counterparts. That doesn't mean you shouldn't network. That just means you have to be more creative about doing it.

A single mom vice president I worked for used lunchtimes with colleagues and employees as her "time out" with other adults. In fact, this was often her only uninterrupted adult conversation time. These lunches were not only a treat for her, enjoying a meal she didn't have to prepare, but also an opportunity for emotional and social support.

My adult students, who are mostly full-time employees returning to college to get their bachelor's degrees, are members of the same cohort throughout the College of Professional Studies program at the University of San Francisco. One night, one student came to class looking forlorn. He told us he had been fired that day. When asked what he was going to do, he said, offhandedly, "I'm gonna learn to play the drums. I've always wanted to play the drums." It turned out that a fellow cohort member played drums in a band and offered to teach this guy to play. Another prime example of networking wherever you find yourself.

You can always carve out time to network. It just may take a little more ingenuity and flexibility to do so. Your network will see you through a downturn. Your network will buoy you in a slump. Your network will energize you. Your network will support you. Your network will celebrate you. Most of all, as you grow in your field, you'll realize that your real job is to network and that the *network is the job*. So, don't be afraid to party your way to the top. Remember, the majority of Fortune 500 executives were "C" students. The time not studying, I'm sure, was spent partying.

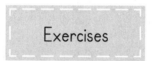

Exercises

1. Make a list of all the colleagues who have left your company or who you have worked with at other companies and are still in the area. Put at least one a month on your calendar for lunch. This forces you to stay in touch with former colleagues and mentors.

2. Identify three prospective colleagues you'd like to get to know better. Invite one a month out to lunch.

3. Identify a sports team you'd like to join or one class you'd like to take every year. Belong to at least one "fun" sports team or take at least one class a year. Identify at least one member you'd like to stay in touch with and do so with quarterly coffee dates.

4. Set aside 30 minutes every week on your Palm Pilot, Blackberry, or calendar for e-mailing or calling

professional associates, former and current colleagues, and mentors. Just a quick call or note to stay in touch. Make sure that these regular ways of "greasing the wheels" of your network are done often without a need or a request. In this way, when you do call with a need or request, the other party will look forward to taking your call.

5. Keep a birthday book. Write all your friends' and colleagues' birthdays in it and set up an e-mail program to send them a note on their birthday. You'd be amazed how touched people are to be remembered on their special day.

6. Send three handwritten thank-you notes a week. Make it a habit.

7. Identify the professional organizations you're interested in and attend their monthly meetings and annual conferences. This is a surefire way to extend your network.

8. Belong to special-interest groups that speak to your passions. Invite members of the group to your home for dessert, barbecues, wine and cheese. Home entertaining expands relationships in a deeper way.

9. Keep a large Rolodex of business cards (I have three) of those you meet, or enter contacts into your Blackberry or Palm Pilot. If you store numbers in a palmtop, be sure to back up your database on your desktop computer. Call or e-mail your contacts periodically. Refer friends to successful lawyers, doctors, contractors, and employers you've worked with in the past. Usually, this network referral system works both ways!

10. Make it a point, as the Dalai Lama advises to "Go somewhere you've never been before at least once a year."

Examples from my list:

2005 19th-century farmhouse in the South of France

2004 South Island, New Zealand; Coast of Oregon

2003 The Hamptons, Long Island, New York

2002 Santa Fe, New Mexico

2001 North Island, New Zealand

2000 Moved to Oakland, California, after 17 years in San Francisco

1999 Puerto Vallarta, Mexico, "Casa Cosmos"

1998 Manhattan, New York City, stay in a midtown apartment

1997 Sydney, Australia

11. Make a list of all the places you've yet to go to that you've always wanted to travel to.

Examples from my list:

❖ Machu Picchu, Peruvian Andes

❖ Pyramids of Cairo, Egypt

❖ Buddhist Temples of Kyoto, Japan and India

❖ Italy, Spain, Greece, Ireland, Sweden, Norway, Hungary

❖ African Photo Safari

❖ Amazon River, Brazil

❖ Synagogues and Churches of Jerusalem, Israel

❖ Mountains of the Himalayas, Tibet

❖ Town of San Miguel de Allende, Mexico

❖ Rainforests of Costa Rica

❖ Waterfalls of Tahiti

❖ Temples of Thailand

Have fun with your list. It need not be a place that'spractical or feasible for you to go to at the moment. Dream big.

12. Learn a new language. Pick one. Take a Berlitz or community college course.

13. Identify 10 committees or boards you'd be interested in serving on and explore the possibilities of being appointed to one.

14. Join a new special-interest group at least once a year. Examples from my list:
    - ❖ Dance class
    - ❖ Hiking club
    - ❖ Writers' group
    - ❖ Glenview/Montclair/Piedmont Supper Club
    - ❖ Glenview Neighborhood Association
    - ❖ Oakland Chamber of Commerce
    - ❖ East Bay Women in Business Network
    - ❖ Bay Area Businesswoman News
    - ❖ Buddhist sangha

15. Take a new class at least once a year. Examples from my list:
    - ❖ Salsa lessons
    - ❖ Swing lessons
    - ❖ Spanish
    - ❖ Weight training
    - ❖ Book readers' club
    - ❖ Playwriting class
    - ❖ Kayaking class

16. Attend cultural events/religious services of cultures and religions other than yours. Examples from my list:
    - ❖ Jewish synagogue
    - ❖ Moslem temple
    - ❖ Dia de los Muertos, Day of the Dead celebration
    - ❖ Kwaanza party

❖   Hanukkah party
❖   Seder
❖   Greek food festival
❖   Italian festival
❖   Gospel music performance
❖   Flamenco dance performance
❖   Chinese New Year's Parade

17. Make a list of all the social situations that make you uncomfortable. Find a friend who is comfortable in those particular social situations and make it a point to go with him or her to one of them at least once a month.

18. Take a course on public speaking, negotiating skills, group dynamics, or interpersonal communications to improve your social skills.

19. At least once every six months, take a day-long workshop on emotional intelligence, improvisation, drama therapy/psychodrama, bioenergetics, or any workshop that enhances your self-awareness and ability to express your emotions.

20. Keep a journal of your emotional reactions to enhance your self-awareness.

21. Play a sport or do an active aerobic exercise every day to improve your ability to handle your emotions productively.

Chapter 5

Expect diamonds. Always keep the jewelry.

The Diva

I always thought I should be treated like a star.

~ Madonna
international pop star

Lessons of a Diva

When Elizabeth walks into a room, heads turn. Two months after we began working together, the long-legged woman with the black curls and fiery brown eyes spun on her red Italian-imported high heels, a rainbow of color gleaming in the neon lights.

"Elizabeth, where did you get that gorgeous ring?"

"Oh, this?"

"Yes, it's stunning."

On her right hand, a teardrop diamond the size of a small button sat in a Tiffany setting of platinum.

"That was husband number three. I had that made years ago," she said, with a wave of her persimmon-painted fingernails.

"The husband you divorced?"

"Why, yes, of course. Always keep the jewelry, honey."

Elizabeth is a diva of the first degree. She buys the best clothes and cars. She never skimps on features: she has four Bose speakers, leather seats, and GPS on the dashboard of her Mercedes-Benz.

She grabs life and won't let it go. She's the only 60-something woman (of course, divas never reveal age or weight) I know who regularly goes out dancing weeknights at the same clubs the U.C.Berkeley students frequent—Ashkenaz, Freight & Salvage, Allegro Ballroom and La Peña. Her Israeli husband (it took him six years to win her hand in marriage) and she start their evenings at 10 and dance salsa and swing into the morning. Once, years after we had worked together and become friends, the saleswoman with the betelnut skin made this confession:

"Elizabeth, you look so young. And, you've never had any work done!" I commented.

"Wrong, darling. Of course, I've had work done." She leaned back in her deck chair laughing. "I had a face lift in my 40s. Don't you remember that week I left Pilot? That wasn't a cruise ship—that was surgery, baby."

"Wow, you can't even tell. One of my friends has a huge scar on her jawline. And, the other's face is frozen in a perpetual 'Howdy Doody' smile."

"Well, I checked this out with my daughter-in-law who works for the American Medical Society. She found me the best plastic surgeon in the city. Of course, he's twice as expensive as all the rest. He told me you have to get your face lifted in your 40s before your face falls. Otherwise, you may get a Cubist look or mad-woman eyes. So, I got it done while I was still at Pilot."

Elizabeth taught me to expect the best. As you might guess, those who expect the best, get the best.

Though a single mother of two boys, Elizabeth managed to complete her degree after her divorce. She lived in a penthouse for 20 years overlooking the San Francisco Bay. When she finally consented to marry her boyfriend, they nearly split up over the terms of the pre-nuptial agreement. She kept the penthouse as a rental and traded up to an architectural wonder in the Berkeley Hills, with 360-degree views of the entire Bay Area from her front deck, living room, and kitchen. Through the architectural portholes, you can see the Golden Gate Bridge, the hills of Mt. Tam, or the water feature of her garden.

The woman whose idea of cooking is takeout insisted on renovating the small kitchen in the designer home. She managed to convince her husband to install a double-dishwasher, large range, zero-clearance stainless steel refrigerator, glass-encased wine storage bin, and recessed beech cabinets. She had him working as the general contractor, securing kiln-dried redwood planks to match the rest of the ceiling and halogen lights in keeping with the house design.

Marriage hasn't slowed Elizabeth down. This summer, she will join her professor-husband at a conference in Northern Italy. Last winter, Elizabeth took a self-directed sabbatical to Spain, dining on tapas and sangria with her cousins in Barcelona at midnight. When Shmuel goes to Poland this spring, Elizabeth will be shopping in Paris until he joins her. This jet-set grandma still makes time for her four grandchildren, sending grateful parents off on cruises to Baja while she chauffeurs the children to the Exploratorium, where she lets them adventure with all the science exhibits their parents would try to direct.

The credo she lives by is, "Don't whine about it! Do something about it. And don't worry about what anybody thinks. If you do what you want, at least one person will be happy!"

Most women, unfortunately, do care what "they" think. So, they sit demurely and ask for little. And little is what they get.

The Salary Discrepancy

A Carnegie Mellon University study of graduate students with master's degrees negotiating salaries found that men's salaries were 7.6 percent greater than women's salaries. Further inquiry uncovered that 57 percent of men and only 7 percent of women had negotiated their salaries. The difference of $4,000 translated to at least half a million dollars less for women than for men over a career lifetime. And because so few women negotiate the offering bid, women rarely received bonuses, stock options, life insurance, extra vacation, gym memberships, parking, and other perks that translated to big dollars over a career lifetime.

Ironically, women's satisfaction with their pay tends to be equal or higher to that of men in similar positions even though women typically earn 24 percent less than men overall. The studies took place in 1978, 1982, and 1999, with the findings remarkably consistent. Scholars believe that women are satisfied with less because they expect less (Babcock and Laschever, 2003).

You Get What You Negotiate

Most women feel that other people control their destiny. So, when they get a new job, they often accept the first offer and assume that there is no room for negotiation. Employers often have more respect for professional and managerial employees who negotiate than for those who settle for these "lowball" offers.

The former director of the Stanford University MBA career placement program urged women to "make your top, your bottom in salary negotiations." So, if pushed to give a salary figure, it's best to say a range of $20K to $30K, with the top salary of $150K to $180K given as a range. You may often not only get your top salary, but even a higher midpoint salary of $165K. Men do this all the time without blinking an eye. But women, concerned about the impression they might make, don't want to appear greedy, so they take the first offer. The problem with this is twofold: You're undervaluing your talent in the eyes of your new employer and increasing your salary by any more than 10 percent a year later might prove impossible. It never hurts to ask.

The Lebanese Stanford MBA career director offered that Americans are not good negotiators for two reasons: They want a *fair* deal and they want the process to be over with quickly. This puts them at a disadvantage, particularly in a global economy, where Asian and Middle Eastern negotiators, for example, feel that it is a triumph to get the best deal, regardless of *fairness,* and shame on the person who does not act on his or her own behalf in dealings. And often, a full day of socializing, with no reference to the deal at hand, is done before even addressing a business contract. In Asian and Middle Eastern cultures, time is elastic and negotiators feel like they have all the time in the world.

When, for whatever reason, you cannot get the salary you want for the job you want, negotiate for more of the intangibles: a percentage of future revenues, stock options, extended vacation, monthly parking, gym memberships, professional memberships, conferences, or travel. Recently I was able to negotiate an additional week's time off for professional development.

Negotiating enhances your chances of getting what you want. More importantly, you walk away from the negotiations with a stronger sense of self-esteem. Soon, you'll feel entitled to more.

In Demand

When you feel entitled to the best, you often get the best. Like the most popular girl in high school, divas attract huge followings. When dating, boys can sense desperation in a girl and often run from it. Divas expect adoration and those around them sense that and give it to them. How do you get to be one of those women in high demand?

Supply and demand. If you're always working late for no extra pay, employers will come to expect that from you. If you're always available to take on the impossible projects, employers will turn to you for them. If you're always willing to meet impossible schedules with no additional budget, you will create an expectation that your bosses will come to expect.

But, on the other hand, if you set limits to what you will and won't do, those around you will perceive your time as "precious" and be grateful to get some of it. If you're not available for every social event during off-work hours, your colleagues will be extra delighted when you do show up for these events. Paradoxically, the less you're available, the more in demand you are. Limited supply. High demand.

Divas cultivate the image of unavailability. Thus, when they deign to spend time with you, you value that time even more than the regulars who are always there for you. The diva may be out getting a manicure and a pedicure during her lunch hour, but the perception is that she is so high-powered that her lunch calendar is always filled. The diva may be taking in a spa treatment, but the perception is that she is high on the Social Register and unavailable for mere mortals like co-workers at the local pub. So, when an Elizabeth shows up at Barney's Brew Pub on a Friday night, heads turn and eyes pop. Once again, the most popular girl in high school is the belle of the ball.

Star Power

The top saleswoman at a Fortune 500 computer company's first subsidiary led by example. At the first sales meeting of the new vice president, an infamous tyrant from the parent company, Christine, showed up in a Vera Wang white linen pants outfit with black Fendi sunglasses two hours late. The Sicilian New

Yorker glared at her, owl-like, behind wire-rimmed glasses. The room went dead silent. Christine pulled off her glasses with a wave of her milk-white hand and said loudly,

"Hi! I'm Christine and I'm from Hollywood!"

Even the vice president had to smile. The only woman managed to undo the tension in a room full of intimidated salesmen.

Another time, Christine had set up a meeting with the executives of a major Southern California bank. When she got to what she thought was going to be a closing meeting between her and the top executive, she walked, instead, into a room of 100 men and women in suits. She had only communicated to the executive by telephone, so she didn't know who he was or what he looked like (this was before company profiles and photographs online). At the end of her presentation, she roared, "So who's gonna' pay for this?" The entire room turned toward the senior executive in the gray suit sitting in the fourth row. Ms. Martin waltzed up to him and presented him with her card. She closed the deal within a week.

Utterly sure of her star power, this top performer got away with outrageous acts that few others could pull off. In fact, her only education was at the Pasadena Center for the Performing Arts. A drama major, her acting career was cut short when her young pilot husband died tragically in an airplane crash. When Christine realized she would have to make a living for herself, she used her stage talent to sell computers. Not only did she drive revenues ahead of the pack, but she also brought many smiles to otherwise dull meetings and off-sites.

Your Belief Becomes Your Reality

Women sell themselves short. Underestimating talents and skills, they aim low. Men, in general, aim high. Some say the difference between a man and a woman being offered a promotion to Chief of Surgery goes like this:

The woman has performed high-risk brain surgery at a teaching university for 10 years. She's supervised over a thousand residents throughout her career. She's presented papers nationally and internationally and been published in the *New England Journal of Medicine*. But, when offered the promotion, her response is, "I'm not really qualified for this new role. I've never managed an entire department. My specialty is really brain surgery. Maybe you should ask Dr. "So-and-So"…"

Dr. "So-and-So," a man, has never managed or supervised residents. He's a competent surgeon, but has only been in his position one year. His response is, "Absolutely. I'm honored that my skills and talents have been recognized and that you have put your faith in me for guiding the future of this institution."

Women are socialized from a very early age to "know their place."

Mommy See, Mommy Do

Socialization starts with gender definition by the age of two. When two adults are in the car, Daddy usually drives. When a light bulb goes out, Daddy usually replaces it. Daddy sits down to the dinner table while Mommy serves. And Daddy controls allowances and major purchases. Is it any wonder that girls grow up to think Daddy controls the destination and safety of the family? Daddy fixes things; Daddy manages and Mommy labors; and, finally, Daddy makes and controls the money while Mommy asks for money from Daddy, even if Mommy is working full-time.

Homemaking is still the largest single occupation for women in the United States. Also, the U.S. has one of the lowest labor force participation rates for college-educated women in the developed world. As recently as 2001, 99 percent of secretaries, 98 percent of child-care workers, 91 percent of nurses, and 82 percent of elementary school teachers were women. Women-dominated fields are, not surprisingly, among the lowest-paid occupations.

Gender gaps in entitlement have not changed since your grandmother's era, with women 35 and younger as likely as their older peers to feel uncomfortable for asking for more than what they have (Babcock and Laschever, 2003).

It's About Money, Honey

Girls are taught not to ask for anything to do with more money. "Nice girls don't ask." Tasks that girls do everyday—dishes, setting the table—are valued less than tasks boys do once a week—mowing the lawn, taking out the garbage. So, starting with home, girls are paid less for what they do. At school, teachers unwittingly reinforce girls' ineptitude by implying that "girls aren't good at math." In the media, that image is portrayed in the slim 11 percent of female financial experts broadcast on the three major television networks.

In a culture that defines status and success by money, to be rendered clueless about numbers and money puts women at a grave disadvantage.

Divas, on the other hand, know the value of a dollar and do not shy away from professions that bring top dollar. It is no wonder that the two divas I knew intimately were saleswomen—because sales salaries outstrip all other professions, including law, medicine, and executive management, in most salary indexes. But, for women to become divas, they have to commit gender violation and risk not being liked by peers who view them as too aggressive. The paradox is divas are so much themselves that people are naturally magnetized to these women who exude confidence.

Control Freaks

A group of psychologists found one important gender difference that keeps women from becoming the divas they were meant to be: "external locus of control." Women score high on external locus of control scales, indicating that women are much more likely to believe that their circumstances are controlled by others, while men believe that they can influence circumstances and opportunities through their own actions. The study, replicated in 14 countries, including Britain, Belgium, the Netherlands, Sweden, Bulgaria, Czechoslovakia, Hungary, Poland, Romania, the former USSR, India, China, Mexico, and Brazil, when controlling for occupational status, reinforced that women felt like victims of their circumstances. Men, scoring much higher on internal locus of control scales, on the other hand, felt like they could make things happen. Men were much more likely to undertake activities to advance their own interests (Babcock and Laschever, 2003).

I Want to Be a Diva

It's easier than you think. There are 10 rules for becoming a diva, but you must do all 10 to achieve this status:

1. Expect the best. Never settle for less.
2. Don't worry what "they" think.
3. Do things that make you happy.
4. Learn to manage your own money.
5. Find a profession that plays to your strengths and pays well, and negotiate the best deal for yourself.
6. Recruit women and mentor girls; there is strength in numbers.
7. Practice taking risks. Take one major risk a year.
8. Take a class that makes you feel like a diva, at least once a year: acting, dancing, improvisational theater, public speaking, opera singing.
9. Model clothes for a charity fashion show at least once in your life.
10. Buy the most expensive "something" you really want at least once a year.

Divas are not selfish; they're self-reliant. Divas don't expect others to make them happy; they make themselves happy. Divas never settle for less; they only accept the best. Divas expect diamonds and always keep the jewelry.

Exercises

1. Pick a store, such as Saks Fifth Avenue, Georgio Armani, or Tiffany's, that you feel is "out of your league." Practice going to that store at least once a month. Once a year, buy one item from the store that you discover, after a year of window shopping, that you really want. Repeat the process every year.

2. Make a list of at least 10 utterly "useless" items you have always wanted for no reason other than you want them. Pick one item from the list and buy it once a year.

3. Write an affirmation of the annual salary you wish to earn. Multiply that salary by 10 and put it up in your office as an affirmation.

4. If you want to buy a house or a second home, join an electronic listing with a major real estate company, and post price range, geography, and features parameters to receive daily listings of available properties in your target areas. Do this whether or not you are ready to buy today.

5. Take a personal financial management course at the local community college, adult education school, or Learning Annex.

6.   Find out about mentoring opportunities at your company or in your community and volunteer at least one hour a month to mentor girls.

7.   Make a list of 10 things you want to accomplish before you die.

8.   Go on a retreat of any kind at least once a year.

9.   Negotiate your next salary no matter how high the offer.

10. Take an inventory of your possessions and jettison all those that don't fit the "best" bill.

11. Before every purchase, analyze what is the *best* product you can buy within your budget.

12. Make a list of 10 things you could do every day, without any outside help, to make yourself happy. Do at least one a day. Examples: Exercise, meditate, read a novel, play tennis, dance, swim, bicycle, hike, walk, sing, write, play a musical instrument, clean out your office, take a hot bath, light a candle, pray, talk to friends on the telephone, meet a friend, write a note or letter, garden, build or refinish furniture.

13. Identify a charity that hosts fashion shows and volunteer to model in one.

14. Identify five risks you could take this year and take one. Start small: go on a weekend trip; hike with a group on a longer hike than you've ever taken; sign up for an adventure bicycle ride.

15. Accept your next extravagant gift with grace and confidence that you deserve it.

Chapter 6

Give them the credit.

The Cheerleader

Begin with praise and honest appreciation.

~ Dale Carnegie
American author

Reach for the Stars

Give me an 'L'. Give me an 'A'.

Before becoming the nicest judge on *American Idol,* Paula Abdul was a pop star, dancer, choreographer, and L.A. Lakers cheerleader. Voted "Most Likely to Brighten Up Your Day," *Miss Congeniality* star Sandra Bullock used to pass the hours away cheering at Arlington's Washington–Lee High School. Born to a renowned opera singer, she and her little sister accompanied their mother on many trips to Europe. No slouch, this smart woman formed her own film production company. An actress with one of the most famous lines in modern movies, "You had me at hello"

(Jerry Maguire), lands multimillion-dollar contracts, but began her career as a cheerleader. The spirit she brought to her roles in *Jerry Maguire* and *Bridget Jones's Diary* led to Renée Zellweger's Academy Award–winning role in *Cold Mountain* in 2003.

She was short, bookish, and hardly the type to try out. But this girl born in Brooklyn, New York, became a cheerleader at James Madison High School. She went on to Cornell University where she was Phi Beta Kappa and made the Harvard and Columbia Law Reviews. She's married to a Georgetown University tax law professor, Martin, and mother to Jane, a professor at Columbia Law School, and James, a producer of classical recordings. Her opinions on sexual harassment changed the face of remedies for women, no longer requiring that severe and pervasive harm be proven, and establishing that a pattern of harassing behaviors created a hostile work environment. Supreme Court Justice Ruth Bader Ginsburg was once a high school cheerleader.

Cheerleaders count among their famous ranks George W. Bush, Samuel Jackson, Michael Douglas, Meryl Streep, Halle Berry, Madonna, Kirsten Dunst, Calista Flockhart, Cameron Diaz, Christina Aguillera, and Katie Couric.

A History of Accomplishment

Starting at Princeton University in 1884, Thomas Peebles, a Princeton graduate, recorded the first yell, done in locomotive style, during a college football game:

Ray, Ray, Ray!
Tiger, Tiger, Sis, Sis, Sis!
Boom, Boom, Boom! Aaaaah!
PRINCETON, PRINCETON, PRINCETON!

Made popular in 1898 by Johnny Campbell, an undergraduate at the University of Minnesota, the first cheerleader stood before a crowd at a football game and directed the yell:

Rah, Rah, Rah!
Skuumar, Hoo-Rah! Hoo-Rah!
Varsity! Varsity! Varsity, Minn-e-So-Tah!

(Neil and Hart, 1979). Since then, Franklin Delano Roosevelt, Dwight D. Eisenhower, and Ronald Reagan all went on to the presidency from, you guessed it, cheerleading.

It is no wonder, then, that one of the first female CEOs, Sallie Krawcheck of Smith-Barney (now one of Citibank's youngest CFOs), was once a cheerleader. She has said it helped her lead and motivate her staff (Professional Businesswomen of California Address, 2003). Blondes aren't the only girls who benefit from a cheerleading background. Myrtle Potter, one of the 50 African-American women in business to watch and the former president of commercial operations during the greatest growth spurt in Genentech history shared the same cheerleader spirit with Sallie Krawcheck on the same podium (Professional Businesswomen of California Address, 2004).

The New Rigor

Cheerleading's not for wimps. Renée Zellweger was a gymnast first and refused to Americanize her name for Hollywood. Most cheerleaders today are required to master gymnastics, dance, choreography, and aerobics. Most practice at least eight hours a week and have to adhere to a fitness and nutrition regime that would daunt most high school and college girls. In addition to tumbling passes, stunts, jumps, dance, and cheer moves, cheerleaders require loud voices, excellent coordination, perfect timing, superb team skills, great attitudes, and good grades. One "cheer dad" noted that while the average person could make a basket, the fundamental building block of basketball, very few can do a back-handspring, one of the simplest skills required of cheerleaders.

Most of all, cheerleaders learn to rally behind the accomplishments of others. Sometimes they console and offer comfort. Other times, they infuse courage and life into a lagging team of players. Win or lose, they always inspire and motivate excellence.

Give *Them* the Credit

The cheerleader's lessons are lessons for life. Girls who learn to cheer on their teammates become the most popular girls in high school. Professional women who applaud their teams go on to succeed in corporate boardrooms.

The women's business conference keynote speakers are wrong. The pundits are wrong. The business schools are wrong. They always tell you to "make sure you get the credit." They tell you that to advance, you must let everyone know of your accomplishments at all times. This is the quickest path to alienating and disenfranchising your staff and colleagues.

The same social rules still apply. Rather than constantly tout your achievements, do the inverse. Give everyone else the credit and accolades will accrue to you, naturally, like long-term interest in a steadily profitable mutual fund. Your bosses, colleagues, and staff will sing your praises for you.

What If My Boss Takes All the Credit?

The risk you run in attributing your successful program or idea to your boss in an effort to include him (most often) in the circle of praise is that he will take all the bows.

That's a valid concern. For 50 years now, men have been presenting others' ideas as their own and have won promotions, compensation, and kudos that should have gone to many worthy women. One way to avoid this is to work for honorable managers, those who praise liberally and attribute their success to their staff.

When you make your executives look good, they will most likely be indebted to you. If you heap praise, you're less threatening. Defenses down, executives are more open to your ideas in the future. The executives look to you as an ally and take that into consideration come salary and promotion time.

Realistically, these kinds of self-assured bosses are rare. In the absence of such a confident leader, what do you do?

Do it like the Army does.
Shoot it. Shoot it.
Do it like the Navy does.
Sink it!

Go Around Him

There are always clever ways around the boss or colleague who grabs the limelight from you. One such colleague, at a higher level and someone to whom I had a dotted line reporting status, tried to wrest a promotion from corporate using my extensive forecasting and strategic marketing work. He asked me to e-mail him the next fiscal year's entire vertical marketing plan, along with an 18-month rolling forecast by close of business that day. Technically, I was supporting him so it would have been insubordinate not to deliver it to him. I knew he wanted this as proof that he was the man for the vice president job that had just been vacated by my former boss and mentor. He was preparing for a meeting with the senior vice president at corporate the following week. So, I gave it to him, but I blind carbon-copied the SVP.

Well, my colleague didn't get the vice president slot; the company collapsed all the vertical markets under another executive. But before the senior vice president retired from the company, he gave me a major promotion and salary increase. Essentially, he created a position and filled the slot with me. That marketing forecast report established my credibility with him, while not overstepping or overtly challenging my colleague.

Lean to the left.
Lean to the right.
Stand up. Sit down.
Fight. Fight. Fight!

You're Only as Good as Your Staff

Any manager who forgets that her success is directly related to her staff's work will fail. To lose the respect, loyalty, and commitment of your staff is to lose your way. You've forgotten what it means to manage. Complimenting your staff takes nothing away from you. In fact, it just shows how good you really are. Their achievements make you look even better.

When you get what it really means to be a manager, you realize that your job is no longer focused on your own individual contributions, but, rather, on the development of your employees. When your staff succeeds, you succeed as a manager.

One horticulturist who manages major landscaping installations at the Marriott Hotels, Adobe, and Cisco Systems was told recently that she was among the most respected managers in her national firm. She was one of only two cited by her staff for her fairness and even-handed management style in a survey of employee satisfaction. An astute senior executive congratulated her, realizing that staff reactions are often the best barometers of management prowess.

What Goes Around Comes Around

The best social opener is to offer a genuine compliment, everything from "what a great haircut" to "that color looks fabulous on you" to "that was an inspiring presentation." This practice costs nothing and often elicits a warm response. Your mother was right: "If you don't have anything nice to say, don't say anything at all."

Your generosity of spirit is always reciprocated. There is a metaphysical rule that says that everything you give comes back threefold. So, if you want praise, send out praise. If you want attention, give attention. And if you want credit, give others credit.

You're the greatest. Yes, you are.
You've got talent. You're a star!

Positive Coaching Works for Kids and Adults

The Positive Coaching Alliance, headed by Jim Thompson at Stanford University, developed the Positive Coach Mental Model and concluded that the optimal ratio of positive to negative coaching remarks should be 5:1, five positives to one negative (Thompson, 2005). Research found that children in the classroom thrive when the plus/minus ratio was 5:1 (Kirkhart, 1972) and that marriages were more stable with the *magic ratio* of five times as many positive feelings and interactions between spouses as negative ones (Gottman, 1994). Players respond most favorably to coaches who engage in greater proportions of supportive and instructional behaviors (*www.positivecoach.org*,1991) than critical and unconstructive ones.

Positive coaching, defined as showing acceptance, reacting positively to mistakes, and giving encouragement and specific positive feedback, has won fans from the pee-wee to the professional ranks. The results are undeniable and can be applied to any situation—work, athletics, marriage, childrearing. The positive coach redefines what it means to be a "winner" and teaches others to focus on a task-mastery orientation rather than on an ego orientation. Ego-driven children compare themselves to others to measure their success. Children with task-involved goals are more likely to feel competent and successful when their performance of specific tasks improves (Nicholls, 1984). The same holds true for adults. If you, as managers and positive coaches, help your staff improve their individual performance and focus on their own plans, rather than set up a competitive environment, you'll create consistent breakthrough performance.

There are three ways to destroy a relationship:

1. Criticism
2. Blame
3. Neglect

And there are three ways to nurture a relationship:

1. Appreciation
2. Affection (Acknowledgment)
3. Attention

These guidelines were originally derived to help couples succeed (DeAngelis and Chopra, 2001), and can help you remember the 3 A's of positive coaching and relationship building: **A**ppreciation, **A**ffection (**A**cknowledgment), and **A**ttention.

Who rocks the house?
We rock the house.
And when we rock the house,
we rock it all the way down!

The Credit Report

One way to both ensure that you get recognition for your results and you give credit to all members of the team who have contributed to a project's success is to produce what I call the credit report.

After every major project—a product introduction, a key trade show, a marketing campaign, a video production—I began summarizing the project in one succinct e-mail. I'd review the goals and objectives, the contributions of the players involved, and the results achieved. I always quantified the results in terms of return on investment or expected ROI. For trade shows, I'd take the number of qualified leads times the company's median sale and put that number over the marketing costs of the show to calculate the expected ROI. In sales, if I didn't make quota, I researched the historical sales in that product line and quantified my annual sales in terms of the percentage increase in sales, year over year. In my first year of sales, while I didn't meet the $1 million quota on a median $25K product sale, I could show that I had increased sales 240 percent and sold to seven of the top 10 banks from a previous base of two of the top 10 banks in one year. That market penetration generated total product sales far in excess of my particular product line quota. I sent out credit reports at the end of every project to all the appropriate executives and members of the project teams.

More Than a Compliment

It's not just a well-worded memo of thanks that people crave, but also a symbol of your appreciation. Even the most buttoned-down senior executives at East Coast banks brightened when I handed them company travel coffee mugs as thank-you tokens for their taking the time to meet with me. One founder argued with me that senior executives weren't impressed with trade show giveaways. That is, until we bought a booth and nobody came when we didn't have "cool stuff" to give away. The next year, we raffled off a shopping trip to New York at the launch of an e-commerce product and quintupled our qualified leads.

Students always appreciate food of any kind. Bring in a pizza to a night class and you're a friend for life. Give away candy for inventive answers to a features/benefits quiz and you're a hero. The highest evaluations of a product training at one company went to a Sun Microsystems trainer who threw out squeeze balls to $5- and $10-million-a-year sales reps who answered questions correctly.

Women love flowers. A bouquet goes a long way to say, "I appreciate you." Men love sporting equipment (stereotypical, but true): a monogrammed bag of golf tees, gym bags, backpacks, polo shirts, or visors. Men and women both love food or wine baskets to share at home or the office.

One particularly desultory Friday afternoon of reducing budgets, just before leaving for Puerto Vallarta, I skipped out to buy the entire marketing staff Haagen-Dazs ice cream and Dole juice bars. The "just because" ice cream break leavened the atmosphere and brought all, including the hard-bitten vice president, together, building an *esprit de corps* that lasted through several more weeks of grueling budget cuts.

Bosses need love, too. After being asked into an important client meeting in Geneva, I gave my boss a card and a Sarah Brightman CD I thought he'd like. When he took me with him to the next company, I gave him a bottle of a limited-edition brandy. Needless to say, the next company he went to he asked me to consult with him and paid me handsomely. He managed to get the board to grant me fully vested options, a benefit normally reserved for full-time employees. Liberal praise of his motivational style and brilliant maneuvering—compliments I believed to be true—enhanced, rather than diminished, my career advancement.

Good Ideas Can Come From Anyone

Never attach title or status to a good idea. Good ideas can and do come from anyone in the organization. John Young, former Hewlett-Packard CEO, knew this when he described the essence of quality: "The person closest to the job knows best how to improve its performance." Every HP paper cup at one time sported the slogan, "Quality: Do It Right the First Time." At coffee hours throughout the company every morning, employees, from production line workers to R&D engineers, from human resources managers to CFOs, drank from the same cup. To do more than just promulgate slogans, Hewlett-Packard formed quality teams of line workers in the fabricators and testers in the lab to improve integrated circuit production at one division in Cupertino. Secretaries to engineers formed task forces to improve their work. The teams saved the division $10 million in one year.

If you are an individual contributor, a manager, or an executive, stay open to all the ideas that come your way. Recognize excellence wherever you find it. Don't be blinded by a title or the lack of one. From the janitor to the receptionist to your departmental administrator to your colleagues to your executives to your customers, listen for the next good idea.

Every great salesperson knows that an executive's administrative assistant is the gatekeeper of his or her calendar, that the receptionist often knows the pulse of a company, and that the janitors can tell you who stays late and who comes in early and who shows up on the weekends. Following the platinum rule, "Treat others as *they* would like to be treated," works for everyone up and down the corporate ladder.

We are the Cougars. We are a team.
We are the winners. That is our dream.
Everywhere we go. People want to know.
Who we are. We are the Cougars.

Just Because

The more you recognize your own gifts, the more you'll be able to recognize talents and skills in others. Giving credit is not something to do to get ahead, although, if you do it often, you will inevitably get ahead. You honor the contributions of others because it's the right thing to do. It feels good.

The paradox is, the more you reflect the light in others, the more the limelight will shine on you. People like to be around people who compliment them and make them feel good about themselves. So, when tempted to toot your own horn, take a breath, step back, and take time to "give *them* the credit."

Let others be your ambassadors. As any good marketer knows, third-party endorsements are always more credible than self-promotions.

Cheer your staff and colleagues on to new heights and when they win, give them the credit. Your "Ra-Ra" will turn into "well done" team excellence, your "well done" into promotions that take you to the top. Sallie Krawchek, one of Citibank's youngest CFOs ever and one of *Forbes* Most Powerful Women, and Myrtle Potter, former president of commercial operations at Genentech, started out as high school cheerleaders and attribute skills learned there—building up the team, cheering colleagues on, staying focused on winning when the going gets tough—to their meteoric personal rise and company performance.

We're headed for the top.
We're solid as a rock.
We can't be stopped, because we're HOT, HOT, HOT!

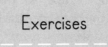

Exercises

1. If one of your staff members wins an award, publish a memo to the company describing the employee's accomplishment.

2. Pay attention to all the contributions of the team bringing about the successful completion of a major project and write a credit report honoring every team member by name and contribution.

3. Bring in breakfast or lunch to your meeting or class.

4. Send flowers to employees, colleagues, and managers for special occasions or no occasion at all.

5. Compliment your colleagues/staff at least once a day.

6. Keep a compliment diary. Note the praises received and the compliments given daily for a month. If you find that there is a dearth of both, step up your efforts to find noteworthy qualities in those you work with every day.

7. Ask people questions about themselves. Then listen to the answers. The next time you see them, refer to their stated interests and concerns.

8. Take a "listening" course. Improve your listening skills.

9. Keep a journal of your daily interactions with your staff, colleagues, and executives for a week. Assess the ratio of positives to negatives. If the ratio is less than 5:1, try shifting the emphasis to increase the positives.

10. Practice "catching your staff doing something right," rather than catching them doing something wrong.

Chapter 7

Be loyal—to yourself.

The Girl Scout

> *The only time I like power is when
> it creates opportunities.*
>
> ~ Billy Jean King
> American tennis champion and
> Olympic coach

The Girl Scout Promise

On my honor, I will try:
To serve God and my country,
To help people at all times,
And to live by the Girl Scout Law.

The Girl Scout Law

I will do my best to be
    honest and fair,

friendly and helpful,
considerate and caring,
courageous and strong, and
responsible for what I say and do,
and to
respect myself and others,
respect authority,
use resources wisely,
make the world a better place, and
be a sister to every Girl Scout.
(*www.girlscouts.org*)

The Modern Girl

She started out making lanyards of shiny red, white, and blue plastic to hold her locker key. She sang silly songs around the campfire and roasted marshmallows until they were black and bubbly at Brownie camp high in the Sierra Nevada Mountains. Amy sold more Girl Scout cookies than anyone else in her troop. She braved banks on Friday afternoons and set up stands outside church on Sunday mornings. Not one peanut butter sandwich or thin chocolate mint cookie was sold by either of her Silicon Valley executive parents. And she did volunteer puppetry with the children at the Lucile Packard wing of Stanford University Hospital. That's why this merit badge holder was shocked when they fired her for being too loyal. She had defended the founder of the subsidiary to the parent company and alerted the corporation's legal team of the dangers of a "stock dump" if they fired the founder outright. She prepared the press release with the general counsel the day before the announcement and did her best to "respect authority," so Amy was stunned when the vice president and general manager fired her the Monday morning of the annual sales meeting.

Amy was loyal. She was true. She did her best to help where needed. After the unceremonious rejection, she floundered for two years as a consultant while the CEO of the subsidiary hosted parties at his Los Altos Hills home and retired early to a wine country estate, where five garages house his vintage car collection. His sky blue Morgan was one of only 12 made every year in England.

It was then that the most decorated Girl Scout in Silicon Valley learned the most important lesson of the Girl Scout Law: "To show respect for myself…"

The Loyalty Oath

Your first loyalty is to yourself. For all the high-minded ideals learned as a Girl Scout, the most precious is a healthy reverence for your own well-being. Your health—physical, mental, emotional, and spiritual—is the most important tool you possess. Without your health, you have no ability to work and carry out your life's mission.

Carol Bartz, executive chairman of the board and former CEO of Autodesk, learned this lesson the hard way. As a high-flying executive during the early days of Sun Microsystem's rise, Carol worked 16-hour days. Scott McNealy, Sun's CEO and founder, handpicked Carol to run some of his most critical operations. It was no wonder, then, that Carol was slated to head up one of the fastest-growing high-tech companies in the San Francisco Bay Area as one of the few women (at the time) to ever lead a high-technology company. Just before starting, Carol made a terrible discovery.

A young mother, Carol faced the worst decision of her life. She had breast cancer and had to decide whether or not to take on the new job while undergoing chemotherapy. Bartz decided to follow a rigorous health regime *and* then take on the role of CEO of Autodesk. In those moments, Carol learned to appreciate the warm and wooly atmosphere of a company that allowed employees to take their pets to work. Those pets became a great source of solace to the healing CEO.

Today, Carol Bartz, still executive chairman of the board and former CEO of Autodesk, is being honored for her contributions to breast cancer awareness. She learned to balance home and work life during that period and continues to do so today. Most of all, she's learned to respect herself, her health, and her family first.

Mission Accomplished

Once I went on a retreat with my church to Point Bonita near the Golden Gate Bridge. As a small group, we were asked to individually sift through 50 verbs and select the five that best applied to our mission in life. From those five, we were asked to narrow our choices down to the one verb that best exemplified our mission in life.

After three days of hiking, contemplating, singing, talking, and collage making, I was able to craft a mission statement for myself that still applies today, eight years later: "To illuminate the Divine in everyone."

Idealistic? High-minded? Yes, but that's what a mission is, a sacred calling. No matter the vagaries of time or the economy, the mission remains as sure as the lighthouse light guiding the parishioners on the rocky coast of Marin that weekend.

"On my honor, I will try to serve God and my country."

Service-Oriented

Whether hosting a MoveOn.org house party or launching a voter registration campaign, Amy served. She volunteered for the Peace Corps after college and built irrigation systems for farmers in the high country of Guatemala even while the country was still fraught with the ravages of civil war. The self-sufficiency she left with the Indian mestizos came back to her in letters and newspaper clippings from the Jesuits still serving in the countryside and comforted her those two years following her Silicon Valley firing years later.

To Help People at All. . .Well, Most Times

After the experience with the first and only firing of her life, Amy learned to modify her zealousness. Like most girls, Amy had learned to put others' needs before her own. As an adult, she finally learned that there is a time to help and a time to let others help themselves. There is a time to put yourself first despite the pressure to do otherwise. And there is a time to leave, well, leave well enough alone.

The occasion to test this newfound self-determination came sooner rather than later. At her next high-tech job, Amy was asked to be part of the transition team that closed a division of 500 employees. Amy, too, was slated to be "redeployed" in the division closure.

Amy helped engineers write their first resumes in 15 years and conducted interviewing and job search workshops for all the employees. She hosted internal job fairs and ferreted out software training programs for the hardware engineers being asked to find other positions within the company. She hosted panels on job relocation for those employees moving out of the Bay Area to outlying divisions in Oregon, Colorado, and the Sacramento Valley. She wrote "Transitions," a weekly e-column on success stories of redeployed employees.

Halfway through the process, with 250 employees placed in new jobs or entirely new positions within the company, Amy began to think about her own future. She had always wanted to work in a more creative department than human resources. She had always wanted to be a part of the faster-paced personal computer division. So, on the day that internal hiring was frozen throughout the company, Amy had just gotten her boss to sign papers releasing her to work for the computer division as an advertising and sales promotion specialist.

Amy jump-started the job-hunting process for 50 percent of the division employees while she, herself, was on the chopping block. She cheerfully went about encouraging discouraged fab operators and testers and disillusioned engineers. But, when push came to shove, Amy finally learned that it was okay to help herself while helping others. And she didn't need to "save the world" in lieu of saving herself. The happy ending to this story is that 90 percent of that division's employees were placed in new jobs within the company within nine months, even though Amy had moved on sooner in the closing-down process.

"I will do my best to be honest..."

This seemed like one law Amy would never violate, even one little white-lie bit. The Catholic school graduate had been taught by the nuns to "tell the truth, the whole truth, and nothing but the truth."

However, even Hewlett-Packard, voted one of the five most ethical corporations in the country (*Business Ethics*, 2002), realized that "telling the whole truth" was slowing the computer business down. So, HP hired an outside training firm and trained its entire marketing staff on the "art of negotiations." All the marketing staff had to submit a self-assessment inventory as part of the pretest for the class. The class was mandatory. The trainers quickly assessed that more than 80 percent of HP staff were either "amiable" or "analytical" on the Wilson Learning quadrant. Amiables like to talk a lot and value relationships over anything else. Analyticals like all the data before making a decision. Either way, neither group proved to be good negotiators. The amiables told too much and never closed. The analyticals talked too little, analyzed too much and never could make a decision in a timely fashion. The third group, and the one to which Amy's dominant style belonged, the expressives, told everything.

Amy quickly learned that the best negotiators say little and reveal nothing of any critical importance. And the first one to break the silence loses the negotiation. So, Amy had to learn to continue to be honest in such a way that did not jeopardize negotiations with her vendors. For example:

Amy:	We want to get the best possible price.
Vendor:	So, how much can you spend on this direct mail piece?
Amy:	Given what we're trying to achieve and the parameters we've discussed, what's your ballpark figure guess?
Vendor:	I'll have to get you a quote. But, it would help if I knew the parameters.
Amy:	The guidelines are 10K run, modest offer, great creative to grab the attention of B2B executive decision makers in the banking industry.

The truth was Amy had plenty of budget, but she wanted the best price. So, though the job was on a rush schedule, she still wanted to achieve her best price objective. Saying nothing about the actual price left her a lot of wiggle room. She got the piece done for less than $10,000 and returned the investment 1,000 percent!

Amy was getting the hang of negotiation. She found it easy to keep her comments short and sweet as long as she could be honest. This method worked equally well inside the corporation.

Vendor:	What's your budget?
Boss:	Why isn't the project finished?
Amy:	I need two weeks.
Boss:	Two weeks! You should have finished a month ago. We need to get this product out to the field. We promised the sales force something this quarter. Amy, how could you screw up such an important deadline?

Amy:	I couldn't make the deadline, Joe. I need two weeks.
Boss:	All right! But, two weeks is all you get! I want it done in two weeks.
Amy:	You got it!
Boss:	You know I'm counting on you.
Amy:	I've got it covered.

The truth was Amy's boss had asked her to do the impossible. She agreed because she was on the fast track for a promotion and thought she might pull it off. However, when the product divisions and third-party vendors slipped their schedules, Amy could not possibly meet her manager's goals. He knew this and, intentionally, set the targets aggressively so that if they slipped a month, he still was well within his own deadlines.

Women generally over-explain. The corporate rule, "No complaints, no excuses," always applies.

Fair's Fair

Women always try to be fair to everyone except, often, themselves. They try to please others at their own expense. Consider the manager who stays late so her staff can pick up their children at daycare. Or the professional who works all weekend so her boss will have the report in London Monday morning when he arrives.

Occasionally, filling in is fair. Making an everyday practice of sacrifice is not only unfair, but your peers and managers also will come to expect that level of sacrifice every time. You'll resent it. And they won't respect you.

"To help where I am needed..."

Volunteering for the Emergency Preparedness Team at your company is a great way to help. Volunteering to chair every

United Way campaign leaves you with too much work to do and not enough thanks. The staff comes to expect you'll volunteer, so they don't. You then become the company doormat, to be tread on, muddy feet and all.

"To be cheerful..."

For sure, if you are going to work in an American corporate environment, you better be cheerful. Optimism is woven into the fabric of the American psyche. To not smile is a cultural violation of such proportions that it could put you on the chopping block in the first round of layoffs. No one likes to be around a sourpuss. Naysayers are avoided like the emotional porcupines they are. When someone asks you how you are, the correct response is "Great!" Anything short of that is suspect. But you need to find those *compadres* with whom you can be utterly honest, expressing the hard feelings you, most of the time, have to hide so you can retain your sanity.

As long as you are working for a company, sing its praises. Look for the things the company does well. Focus on the positives. And never announce your departure before it is a "done deal." As long as you're with a company, "Love the One You're With" (Stills, 1970).

Heart Attack Waiting to Happen

Heart attacks strike 440,000 American women a year, burying nearly 250,000, more than stroke, lung, and breast cancer combined. Two-thirds of women who die from heart attacks have no warning symptoms of any kind. Heart disease, not cancer, is the number one killer of American women (American Heart Association, 2005).

Cardiologists (Friedman, 1985) have identified the personality traits of women most likely to suffer heart attacks as the Type A Personality:

1. Stressing while waiting for anything
2. Doing multiple tasks at one time, instead of doing one thing at a time
3. Taking everything too seriously
4. Perfectionism
5. Pursuing everything equally intensely, from picking a dress for Saturday night to climbing Mt. Everest

Learning to be cheerful, relax, and have fun is a lifesaver. Transcendental meditation at least 20 minutes a day (Bloomfield et. al., 1975) and aerobic exercise lower blood pressure and reduce the risk of heart attack and stroke.

The Harvard University longitudinal study of 11,130 graduates (1916-1950) that followed the group for more than 40 years found that physical activities that burn 1,000 to 2,000 calories a week lower the risk of stroke by 24 percent and caloric burn of 2,000 to 3,000 calories a week lower the risk by 46 percent. The latter amounts to a brisk, hour-long walk, five days a week (Lee and Paffenbarger, 1998). Other Harvard studies found that aerobic exercise, more than any other activity, including diet, lowered the risk of heart attack more than any other factor.

"To be friendly and considerate..."

Girls are trained to be thoughtful. Women grow up to be the biggest purchasers of greeting cards, wrapping paper, and gift items. This thoughtfulness never goes out of style. Companies ranked among the 100 "best" every year by Moskowitz and Levering exemplify friendliness, consideration and respect. Washington Mutual prides itself on its friendly atmosphere. Macy's dropped the walls to competing perfume counters. Nordstrom accepts any returns, no questions asked.

"To be a sister to every other Girl Scout..."

It is time women learned to support one another at work. Andrea Jung had the CEO of I. Magnin retailer as a mentor before Jung herself became the CEO of Avon Products. World Savings employees have Marion Sandler, co-CEO of Golden West Savings and one of a handful of women CEOs, to fight to add women to the board of directors when she looked around the boardroom and saw only white male faces.

Unfortunately, these are the exceptions, not the rule. The "good old boys' network" is still a network of "boys." Sometimes, women are your own worst enemy. Consider Carly Fiorina, one of only nine women Fortune 500 CEOs in 2005, before being ousted in February of 2005. When appointed by the Hewlett-Packard board of directors in 1999, she claimed that her appointment proved "there is no glass ceiling." Fortunately, she admitted later at a Commonwealth Club press event that this was a mistake and that she was wrong about that comment. Though women make up more than 50 percent of the Fortune 500 workforce, they make up less than 2 percent of the CEO ranks.

The burgeoning growth of women's professional organizations signals a change in the air: National Association of Female Executives, National Association of Women Business Owners, Professional Businesswomen of America. Finally, women are in positions to hire and support one another with mentoring, networking, and succession planning.

"To respect authority..."

Through the military and football, men learn early to play by the rules. Despite any illusion of democracy, corporations are hierarchical. Don't be fooled by the khakis and open collars. The CEO is still the chief and your boss still writes your performance review. A healthy respect for authority guarantees your survival and advancement. Men willingly submit to the rigors of authority. Women often rebel and create unnecessary stress.

"To use resources wisely..."

Whether cutting costs or saving money with green policies and global economies of scale, the woman who knows the numbers wins. The Hopi say to "make every decision for the next seven generations." The millionaire next door clips coupons and resoles his shoes. If you treat your company budget with the same parsimony, you'll be rewarded with greater budget responsibility and more resources.

"To protect and improve the world around me..."

The good corporations do no harm. The great corporations make an indelible contribution to the greater good of society. That's why the real visionaries always have a mission greater than themselves. Charles Schwab wants to help "everyone become financially independent." Fannie Mae wants every American to own the American dream. Leapfrog wants to make literacy a right for every child.

Recently, Leapfrog made good on its tag line, "to learn something new every day," by donating LeapPads to the uneducated women of Afghanistan to help them learn about healthcare.

Whether Mothers for Peace in Northern Ireland, or Tibetans under house arrest by the Chinese for standing up against the brutal slaughter of a nation, or feeding the poorest of the poor in India, or supporting Indian rights in Guatemala, women have gone to great lengths to improve and protect the world. For this, at least four women have won the Nobel Prize for Peace in the last 20 years.

"To show respect for myself and others through my words and actions..."

Looking good is not just a fashion statement. It's a way of saying you love yourself and want to look your best. Speaking without swearing is a way to show respect. When all the sales reps on Long Island were using expletives in every other sentence, my non-swearing response stopped these New Yorkers in their tracks.

A priest once told me to avoid "triangulations and gossip," the trademarks of political intrigue and diabolical consequences. Never get in the middle of a disagreement between two people. Never gossip if the discussion of the non-present third party harms the third party in any way.

"On my honor" will keep your faith in troubled times. The Enron accountant who alerted the executives to shady accounting processes can sleep well in her own bed tonight. When you're loyal to yourself, you remain faithful to your own ideals. That kind of loyalty is priceless.

Exercises

1. Make a list of all your best attributes. Next to each one, write the names of those in your circles who share this attribute. Make it a point to compliment them the next time you see them.

2. List all your colleagues. Name one outstanding trait in each one of them. Try bringing out that trait every week in one fashion or another.

3.   Make a list of all the people in your department, on your floor, in your building, and if the organization is small enough, in your company. Practice memorizing their names by calling them by name every time you see them for the next eight weeks (it takes eight weeks to form a habit). Consider name tags for your next company-wide meeting or permanent name tags as a way to reinforce learning everyone's name.

4.   The next time you lead a meeting or a class, go around the room and have all the people introduce themselves and name their favorite sport or say what they would be if they were a force of nature and why they chose that phenomenon. (Another option: Ask what animal they'd be if they were an animal and why.) It's a way to both reinforce their names and to pique everyone's curiosity about one another.

5.   Regularly host brown-bag luncheons for your staff and cross-functional teams. Conduct a brainstorming session as though it were an executive strategic planning session. Write up the best ideas and choose one a quarter to act on as a team.

6.   Send personal thank-you notes for a job well done or an effort on your behalf or a big customer win.

7.   Include bosses in your gift-giving and thank-you notes and compliments.

8.   Take a yoga, Pilates, or t'ai chi class. Make time for yourself during the workweek to recharge and rejuvenate yourself.

Chapter 8

Mentor knows best.

The Apprentice

Keep away from people who try to belittle your ambitions. Small people always do that, but the really great make you feel that you, too, can become great.

~ Mark Twain
American writer

"You're Fired!" (Donald Trump, *The Apprentice*, 2006)

Despite its popularity as one of reality TV's top three shows, *The Apprentice* with billionaire Donald Trump represents the underside of apprenticeship. Any mentor-apprentice relationship that leaves you feeling less than the brightest and the best that you are represents the kind of relationship you should avoid.

I was once offered a prestigious fellowship from a Midwestern Big 10 university. The only catch was that the fellowship was contingent upon reporting to one of the most disliked professors on campus. As was the case with many well-known experts in his field, this professor was also editor of my discipline's national journal.

So, enticed by the promise of publication and the highest stipend available to this working-class student, I went for and won the prestigious fellowship.

After a night of tossing and turning and getting up to drink warm milk and honey, herbal tea, and brandy, I decided to reject the fellowship for which I had just signed up the day before. I didn't want to wind up in the emergency room with a bleeding ulcer like this professor's last graduate assistant. I didn't want to be one of the three secretaries who quit in one year. I didn't want my life turned upside down by the midnight calls on the weekends or the appropriation of my work as his own that this professor was notorious for doing. In a Ph.D. program, your adviser holds the key to your academic future. Though the prize was great, the price was too high. I was no naïve protégé, willing to be publicly humiliated. I was no novice, willing to slave in the background for the glory of a rather mediocre scholar reaping the benefits of his hapless teaching assistants. I rejected the fellowship the next day, sanity intact, and returned to California with my master's degree where my life of service took a corporate turn.

Access

While working as the independent living skills coordinator of a center for independent living for disabled adults, I formed a bond with one of the disabled board members when I co-chaired the first able-bodied/disabled women's conference ever hosted in California. Although in a wheelchair with multiple disabilities, this man was brilliant. Hewlett-Packard hired him as its communications director, and we kept in touch with the occasional phone call and lunch. He mentored me through several sticky political situations at the nonprofit agency. One day, he mentored me right into his job at HP.

He had been offered a promotion to corporate and wanted to leave his position in good standing, so my mentor now recommended me for my first corporate job. I had long since left the nonprofit agency where we had met and was working as the senior disabled coordinator for a government agency going through severe budget cuts. My ongoing, non-threatening role as apprentice to this brilliant community leader led me, unwittingly, into my first corporate job at one of the most admired companies in America at the time, Hewlett-Packard. After a grueling set of three day-long interviews over the course of a month, HP hired me as my mentor's replacement, though I had very little direct experience for the job. In fact, a poem included in an eclectic writing portfolio was one of the deciding factors for one member of the team who was not, at first, convinced I was the right person for the job.

At Hewlett-Packard, it takes a long time to get hired and everyone on the team must vote *yes* for you, but once you're hired, it's hard to get fired. Hewlett-Packard invests in its employees, up front, and then commits to their success. Fortunately for me, my first foray into corporate life was a great one.

Mentor Knows Best

We no longer live in the world where Kitten is Daddy's favorite little girl in *Father Knows Best*. A man in a crisp white shirt, red tie, and gray suit doesn't rescue us from every dilemma we get ourselves into at work.

But, as most successful men have found, mentors are necessary for your advancement. Sam Palmisano, IBM CEO, had Lou Gerstener, former CEO. Dr. Ed Catmull, president of Pixar, has Steve Jobs, CEO and chairman of the board of both

Pixar and Apple Computers. Nicholas Cage, award-winning actor, has his uncle, award-winning director Francis Ford Coppola. Michael Jordan had Coach Phil Jackson. Tiger Woods, pro golfer, has his dad.

The Glass Ceiling Report (1995) identified the lack of mentoring as one of the two major obstacles to women's success. The other, not surprisingly, was the lack of informal networking. Mentors, as any young up-and-comer knows, are the key to the promotions and plum assignments given to protégés.

A few women have mastered the art of seeking and following a positive mentor's advice and their successes are notable.

Golden West Financial Corporation and World Savings directors have co-CEO and cofounder, Marion Sandler. Judith Jamison, choreographer, had Alvin Ailey. Merce Cunningham, choreographer and dancer, had Martha Graham; Twyla Tharp, choreographer and dancer, had Merce Cunningham. Georgia O'Keeffe, painter, had Alfred Stieglitz, her photographer-husband. Chef Joyce Goldman had Alice Waters, founder of California cuisine showcase restaurant in Berkeley, Chez Panisse.

But many more women do not enjoy the benefit of mentors. Nearly half (47 percent) of all women executives say exclusion from informal networks of communication holds women back from top management positions (Catalyst, 1996). It is through those informal networks of communication that men often bond with prospective mentors. The country club Saturday afternoon golf foursome looking for a fourth can lead to an executive mentor or business partner as it did for Bill Bankert and Randy Gussman, the founders of Zantaz, a market leader in secure electronic transactions. Attending baseball games can lead to business deals as it has for Peter Liebowitz, proud owner of four box seats behind home plate to the Oakland A's games.

Best Sales Advice Ever

Along the way in my career, I've been fortunate to have had many mentors. One came to me in the oddest of ways. He was our vice president of technical sales support and could not have been less like me in every way. Frank Piedad was a 58-year-old father of six grown children, married to a Greek immigrant. His parents were Czech and Spanish. Every day, he wore a gray suit and a white shirt and tie and never changed his hairstyle. Frank took a flight to every big deal a sales rep needed him for, whether he was anywhere near the city in his myriad travels or not. Analytical to a fault, he rarely made swift decisions and could dissect any technical problem down to the integrated circuit. A high school graduate, he had no college degree and was a self-made man.

One day, just a week after taking on the biggest challenge of my career to become a national account executive, Frank walked into my office. Seeing the down look on my face, he said, "What do you think you need to succeed in sales?"

"I need qualified leads, a bigger product price point, and the cooperation of all the local sales reps to sell my product through in the territories."

"Not at all."

"What do you mean, Frank, not at all?"

"There's only one thing you need to know to sell—and that is, 'when you get a yes, shut up.'"

He said this, Yoda-like, and walked out of my office. I didn't know what he meant until six months later, when selling a big deal to Chemical Bank of New York, I had to shut up and take the order before I lost the deal by overselling.

What is important is not so much the advice, although this advice was something no Harvard MBA would teach me, but the willingness to learn from the experiences of others. Since that day, I have adopted the Suzuki way of being, "Zen mind.

Beginner's mind." This Buddhist leader taught Americans to always maintain a fresh and somewhat innocent approach to life. Then, you will continuously learn and adapt as you go. One of the tricks to finding a mentor is to recognize one when you see one.

The Problem for Most Women

Only eight women, or 1.6 percent, are CEOs of Fortune 500 companies (*National Association of Female Executives,* 2005). So, while men have many "buddies" in high places to choose from, women have few. That's why most successful women in Corporate America learn valuable lessons from male mentors.

They "play by the rules." They go along with their mentor's advice. They take risks. They take advantage of informal opportunities to network with senior executives, customers, and business partners. They, if they can, find women role models as Andrea Jung, CEO of Avon Products, did when she made her first cross-country move to work for a woman mentor at the high-end I. Magnin department store in San Francisco. When they can't find a woman high enough in the organization or secure enough in herself, they seek male mentors as Carol Bartz, former CEO of Autodesk, did when she shadowed Scott McNealy, Sun Microsystems co-founder and CEO, before going off to take the helm of her own high-tech company.

How Do You Crack the Code?

Finding a mentor is one of the pursuits (sales and starting a business being two others) where being aggressive pays off.

One time, I was invited spontaneously by the most senior executive at a sales training and customer conference in Geneva to come to a customer dinner. I was the only woman invited to this prestigious, intimate meeting at a five-star restaurant. Although I had been participating in a team-building exercise as part of an intensive sales training program with my headquarters' colleagues, I risked their ire to attend the customer dinner.

The next day, the entire team was mad at me for deserting the nearly all-night session to prepare for the mock client presentation. But that meeting with a top Euro telecom company proved more strategic to my career than any in-house training session ever. That dinner solidified my relationship with the senior vice president of my area and secured me two promotions at that company, one pull to another start-up with that executive, and a major consulting job with that executive at a third company. Stepping out of my gender role of pleasing the group was hard to do, but it proved the right choice in the long run. Although Peter Liebowitz was a couple of levels up from me, I not only recognized him as a mentor, but followed him to two other companies, where he got the board of the last one to grant me fully vested options normally reserved for founders, senior executives, and board members.

There are three things you must do to find a mentor:

1. Ask.
2. Don't stop until you get a *yes*.
3. Pursue the mentor relationship even after your mentor leaves your company to go somewhere else.

Givers Attract Givers

The mysterious irony of the mentor-apprentice relationship is that the apprentice often gives back to the mentor as much as she gets.

At a book pre-release presentation, Gloria Steinem, "mother of the woman's movement" and co-founder of *Ms.* magazine, said that younger women gave her more than she felt she gave them with their enthusiasm, open views based on their expanded possibilities, and confidence in doing things "we never did in the 60s" (Steinem, 2004). Steinem always gave freely of her time and wisdom, and her positive approach made her attractive to leaders around the world.

Why Women Need Help

Women, generally, live longer than men, are more likely to live alone in later years, and will probably live in poverty, because nearly 70 percent depend on Social Security for part of their retirement income and nearly 20 percent depend on Social Security for all of their retirement income.

Today, 35 percent of women in the United States are single, and the number remaining single throughout their lives is growing.

On average, women put 40 to 50 percent less into savings, investments, and retirement accounts than men do. And 80 percent of all women workers will have to continue working, at least part-time, after they "retire" to maintain even a modest lifestyle (Evans and Avis, 2003).

Service women employees are less prepared than men, financially; these women are still making only $0.77 on the $1. Over the course of a lifetime, a woman's risk of living in poverty is double the risk for a man.

And the risk is not just for poor and undereducated women. Stanford University has lost gender discrimination lawsuits brought by women in its medical school and is under investigation by the U.S. Labor Department over claims of discrimination in the hiring and promotion of equally or more qualified female faculty; female professors at Stanford hold only 19 percent of all tenure-track positions.

The way out for women is not only to individually seek and learn from mentors but also to work for companies and institutions with a commitment to advancing women and paying women equally.

In Good Company

You know you're in good company when a company's top earners are women, a company has strong female representation on its board of directors, and the company boasts a formal mentoring program to advance women.

An Accenture study of 483 senior executives found that the torrent of layoffs from 2001 to 2004 have persuaded 80 percent of business leaders that "people issues" are more important now than in 1998 (Management Mentors, 2004). And 70 percent of executives feel retaining existing talent is "far more important than acquiring new blood." HR.com estimates that the cost of a replacement worker is two to three times the cost—approximately $50,000 for the typical worker—of a returned worker (*www.hr.com*).

To create a formal mentoring program, the following goals are generally set:

❖ Professional development
❖ Succession planning
❖ Talent retention
❖ Diversity
❖ Breaking the glass ceiling

In almost all formal mentoring programs, the following guidelines will help:

❖ Formally, the apprentice's manager is not the mentor.
❖ The relationship is focused on development outside the mentoree's area of work.
❖ The mentor takes a personal interest.

❖ The relationship is initiated by the mentor or matched by the organization.

❖ Informally, managers may mentor select employees.

Companies that have set up formal mentoring programs with great success include:

❖ Hewlett–Packard

❖ IBM

❖ Home Depot

❖ Quaker Oats

❖ Charles Schwab

While the Boys Play, the Girls Slave Away

Early on, boys learn to play. They never stop. First, Little League and Pop Warner football. Then, league soccer and basketball. Then, high school and college intercollegiate and intramural sports. Just because they leave the locker room behind when they don a suit for corporate life doesn't mean they leave play far behind.

Whether on the golf course, in the local bar, at the yacht club or in the clubhouse, men have easy access to the power brokers. There are no barriers to admission. That's why Louise Renne, San Francisco City Attorney, sued the Olympic Club, a bastion of male power and dominance for more than 100 years, and won admission to the prestigious club's golf course and facilities for women. Because 90 percent of the Fortune 500 CEOs (Woo, 2002) play golf, access to the same tee times and country clubs is essential to forming those informal relationships that lead to those mentoring opportunities.

Girlz Rule

In the old paradigm, only men could be mentors. That's because only men were in high enough positions to properly mentor you to success. I must confess that 90 percent of my mentors have been men; few women were either high enough in the organization or secure enough to properly guide and coach me.

One top saleswoman, however, did take the time to show me the ropes. One day, when chatting about my new sales position, I said boldly, "I know I'm going to be successful because I'll work harder than any of those other sales guys." She stopped me dead in my tracks and retorted, "Don't work harder, work smarter. One half hour of concerted effort is better than eight to 10 hours of wasted effort."

"Yeah, right." I thought to myself. That's just another cliché. I actually thought she might be threatened by me because I was the only other female sales account executive and was just passing me off with platitudes.

I thought that until I went on my first sales call with her and a vice president in Seattle, Washington. Whenever I'd seen her in sales meetings, she always appeared ditsy and flirtatious. The morning before the closing sales call, she called a 7:30 a.m. meeting with the sales team of technical and executive support. She went over a 50-page Request for Proposal (RFP) with the alacrity of a jaguar, focusing on the three key criteria for selection and the three main objections to our company's solution being chosen. Her meeting lasted 30 minutes but was one of the most concerted meetings I'd ever attended at that company.

Then, three hours later, we went by taxi to the customer's headquarters. Christine Martin took her $400 moss green suede shoes off and put them in a brown paper bag and walked in the rainy parking lot in leather loafers. When we got to the lobby, she made a beeline for the restroom where she freshened up her Chanel suit and matching suede high heels. When she walked out of the bathroom, every head in the lobby turned.

Once in the customer boardroom meeting of 30 technical geeks, executives, and recommenders, a major glitch occurred. In the middle of Ms. Martin's presentation, a techie in the back of the room, eager to shoot down her security argument in favor of choosing her high-end ATM card activation product, poked a major hole in her encryption theory of her presentation. Christine was never technical. But she didn't miss a beat when she went over to the top customer executive in the room and asked for his wallet. The room went silent. The stunned executive pulled out his weather-beaten leather wallet and handed it to her. Her vice president of sales out from New York was ashen-faced. She took out the customer's ATM card and ran it twice through the Card Activation and PIN Selection (Atalla CAPS) machine to prove the techie wrong in his fears of stolen identity. In a loud voice, she said, "So what?" By the break, Christine and her vice president were closing the multimillion-dollar deal in the hallway with the admiring customer who had just experienced a graphic illustration of the value of the system.

From my dear mentor who, sadly, died of cancer at 48, I learned the real meaning of "work smart, not hard." Long before that phrase became a cliché, I had the privilege of observing a master salesperson at work who took the time to coach a neophyte.

The first thing I thought of when Christine died was, now, how can I mentor other young women and men coming through?

The "Old Girls" Network

Finally, there is one.

Jackie Spier, California State Senate, the associate who was wounded leaving an investigation of Jonestown with then-Lt. Gov. of California, Leo McCarthy, spearheaded the Professional Businesswomen of California (PBWC) annual conference. Now in its 17th year, the PBWC affords women in all the major northern and southern California regions an opportunity to bond with other professional women and executives. The conference draws inspiration from such accomplished women as Olympia Dukakis, actress and theater company director; Sallie Krawcheck, former chairman and CEO of Smith-Barney and current CFO of Citibank;, Sheila Heen, author; and Brandi Chastain, gold medal Olympic soccer player.

The PBWC created a blueprint for success. Hewlett-Packard, Chevron, Genentech, Charles Schwab, and other businesses sponsor tables of women attendees from their companies. Companies sponsor high school girls to attend, on scholarship, every year. A young women's program keeps the conference alive and enlivening. Trade shows, medical self-assessments, book fairs, keynotes, and workshops inspire 5,000 to 6,000 women each year in every major region in the state.

The opportunities for mentoring and finding mentors are endless. The women who come to present come willing to offer their services as role models and mentors to the next generation of women leaders.

"When the Student Is Ready, the Teacher Appears" (Buddhist Adage)

When you are truly ready to learn and grow and even hear some things you don't want to hear about your strengths and your weaknesses, then you are ready to be an apprentice to a mentor. You're only as good as the people you choose, so choose wisely. Be ready to enter into one of the most rewarding, challenging, and growth-producing relationships of your life. When you're ready to fly on your own, don't forget to coach the next group of fledglings who come up behind you. As everyone knows, what goes around, comes around.

Exercises

1. Make a list of all possible mentors in your current company. Take each one to lunch until you find a mentor you like.

2. Identify at least three professional organizations you might join to find a mentor. Select one and become an active member, including serving on committees and boards.

3. Attend professional businesswomen's conferences and use e-mail, phone calls, notes, and informational interviews to follow up with the role models you meet.

4. Assess your next career move and find a mentor who is currently in that role to work with informally.

5. Identify 10 companies in your geographical area with formal mentoring programs. Find out if one of them would be a better fit for you and join the program once you get there.

6. Learn to play a sport—golf, tennis, sailing, skiing— where you might find executive role models.

7. Join a board and take a different board member out to lunch every month for a year.

8. Ask your boss for suggestions of mentors and follow up with informal meetings.

9. Keep in touch with mentors even after you no longer need them.

10. List 12 ways you can nurture your current mentor relationship and do one a month.

Chapter 9

Savor the experience.

The Chef

The mere sense of living is joy enough.
~ Emily Dickinson
American poet

"Bon Appetit"

Julia Child (*www.pbs.org*) closed every cooking show with the phrase "Bon appetit." The American cook turned French chef extraordinaire, exemplified the woman's role in the kitchen. Julia was the keeper of secrets, including the chicken that fell on the floor and still went back in the oven and the basil that came from the store, not from the garden, ground into pesto. No low-fat advocate, Julia put real heavy cream into her crème brulee and real butter into her hollandaise.

Along with Jacques Pepin (*www.jacquespepin.net*), her lifelong friend and collaborator, Julia Child showed America how to savor the experience. The two chefs would pour a full-bowled glass of Pinot Noir, Chardonnay, or Cabernet Sauvignon and sit down to every meal they had just prepared. And from the look of them, it was clear they really ate every bite they created.

The Cook's Tour

Every woman knows the meaning of the cook's tour. It is the backdoor trip through the kitchen. Women are masters of the cook's tour. Your lives take twists and turns you never imagined. Women, by definition, are natural-born multitaskers: wives, mothers, students, employees, and entrepreneurs.

Whatever your role, don't feel bad about taking side trips and detours throughout your life. A move to the West Coast might mean finding the love of your life. Two years off to raise your first baby might be the happiest and most fulfilling years of your life. Leaving your job to go back to school mid-career might be the best career move you'll ever make.

The spins and off-road travel you do may bring you the greatest joys of your life. Maybe that is why more college-educated women in America are staying home than at any time since 1950 (Babcock and Laschever, 2003). Stepping off the corporate fast track to raise a young child or sail around the world could be the best use of your time.

One Hewlett-Packard general manager took a year-long sabbatical to sail around the world. She left at the top of her game and returned refreshed and enriched by the experience of a lifetime. So, don't take the same old route to the top. Take the cook's tour. You may be much happier for having explored behind the scenes and off the beaten track.

Keep It Fresh

Every year, go somewhere you've never been before. For me, this has become a mantra. So, one year, I visited the Oregon Coast, staying in a beach house and making the road trip throughout northern Oregon, stopping at a salmon fish stand in Waldport, a farmer's market in Eugene, a college hangout in Corvallis, and the Chinese Gardens in Portland. This year, I ventured to the South Island of New Zealand to sail and hike Arthur's Pass, adventures I'd yet to explore there. The place you've never been before can be as near as your neighborhood church or as far as New Zealand. We also wound up in the South of France, touring from a 19th-century farmhouse in a small village named Chelieu. It doesn't matter where you go; it only matters that you go somewhere you've never been before.

To keep it fresh, learn a new skill every year. Pick something you've always wanted to do and do it. This year, it was ballroom dancing for me. Learn a new language. Go to a country where they don't speak English. Try a homestay in a foreign country instead of a sanitized American hotel. (I practice what I preach, staying in a home-stay pottery studio on Waiheke Island in New Zealand and a farmhouse in the Rhone-Alps region of France.)

Learn new computer software programs that enhance your productivity and fun. For some, that means a digital camera and a program to create holiday cards and invitations. For others, it means a new graphics program to enhance your PowerPoint presentations. Take on new jobs within your current position. Expand your role. Try new industries. Never stand still or the world will, indeed, pass you by, as 450,000 laid-off Californians in the nine-county San Francisco Bay Area found in the recession of 2000 through 2004.

Fresh is more than a bagel or berries in season. Fresh is a way of living. From changing your route to work to changing your workout routine, keeping it fresh keeps you young, vibrant, and as alive as the organic broccoli in your garden.

The Cook for All Seasons

Alice Waters (*www.chezpanisse.com*), the founder of Chez Panisse restaurant in Berkeley, California, and author of several cookbooks, spawned a new way of cooking in the United States, aptly named California cuisine. I say aptly because California grows more fruits and vegetables than any other state. From berries to apples, walnuts to apricots, asparagus to avocado, broccoli to lettuce, and citrus to rice, California is the fruit and vegetable basket of the country. Alice Waters insisted on fresh, natural, organic, in-season produce for better-tasting food and greater nutrition. Her style of cooking inspired many chefs who came after her to infuse their customers' lives with variety, health, and longevity. That's why Prince Charles, an organic farmer enthusiast for 20 years, toured with Waters when he visited the San Francisco Bay Area in 2005.

You can apply the lessons of Alice Waters's kitchen to your own life. Honor the seasons of your life, all of them, including the mid- and late-life paths. Seniors who stay involved have been shown to be less depressed and have sharper memories and better cognitive skills than those who retire from life. Women who read cultivate a lifetime learning approach that sustains them throughout all phases of their careers.

Some say that in youth, we learn; in mid-life, we earn; in senior years, we return. Because the number of careers for the average person is now five, these cycles will repeat themselves over and over throughout your lifetime. So, become a chef for all seasons.

Au Natural

Like unadorned fruits and vegetables in season, the corporate professional who is naturally herself is the most captivating of all. The more parts of yourself you can claim at work, the happier and more integrated you will be. From comfortable shoes to light makeup, the better you feel in your body, the more relaxed, flexible, and likeable you're apt to be at work.

Stone Ground

Every woman in Corporate America who succeeds will learn to do the hard stuff—budgets, managing people, and downsizing. The professional woman raised on white bread—individual contribution, no budget responsibility, no span of control—will often be unable to withstand the rigors of change within organizations. So, steel yourself with the mettle of tough challenges and you will come out stronger and more robust. Like the whole grains in stone-ground wheat, your value will be greater for having stood up to the rigors of corporate life.

Organic

For women, it's natural to grow organically. The thicker corpus callosum that unites the right and left hemispheres of the brain ensures that women will think both intuitively and linearly. Holistic thinkers, women are not deterred by the rigid need to follow a straight line to the top.

One corporate executive retired early and returned to the local community college to become a landscape architect. She traded her New York trips across country for trips to the local nursery. Formerly a six-figure earner, she went down to minimum wage to master a new craft altogether. She's never been happier, digging her hands into mulch, selecting cyclamen and daffodil bulbs, planting makeshift gardens for "staging" homes for sale. Soon after she began her apprenticeship, friends and friends of friends have asked her to redesign their backyards or stage their front yards for home sales. She now has to turn away business.

Another woman, an executive speechwriter for the CEO of a Fortune 500 company, left her "cushy" corporate job to pursue a teaching credential after undergoing a year of surgeries, chemotherapy, and radiation for a serious cancer contracted in her fifteenth year of corporate life. After completing an intensive two-year program, she landed a job as an elementary-school teacher in one of the best schools in California. She traded opulent product launch parties with vintage wines and catered sushi bars for down-home potlucks and homemade decorations in the teacher's lounge and has never been happier.

Some women step off the corporate track forever. Some merely take a detour that prepares them for the next leap forward. As a woman, organic growth and development happens as the interplay of life circumstances take you in whole new directions.

The trick is to remain open to the call of your own heart. Then you will water all the parts of yourself and not find, as one man did on his deathbed, "I had gotten all the cookies in life— nice home, expensive car, lavish trips, kids in college, great wife, great job, lots of money—when I finally realized that life was the cookies" (Remen, 1996).

Made from Scratch

As cookies made from scratch taste better than store-bought ones, women who mix talent with hard work and good relationship building offer better fare to their employers. Because women rarely have access to the "good ole boy" network, they must rely on the raw materials—brilliance, technical skills, people skills—to advance.

Spice It Up

Don't be afraid to "add a little spice" to your interactions at work. One CEO I worked for told me he always read my e-mails. When I asked him why, he said, "They're never dull. You spice them up with humor, yet get right to the point." A dry memo about a budget request can be leavened with a joke. A dull report turned colorful with stories and tidbits of information can make the busiest executive want to read your e-mail.

Instead of turning out boring PowerPoint text messages slide after slide, follow the rules of good public speaking (Kawasaki, 2004):

- ❖ Use no more than 15 slides, preferably 10.
- ❖ Open your speech with a strong story, metaphor, or shocking statistic.
- ❖ Sprinkle humor, preferably self-deprecating humor, throughout your talk.
- ❖ Close with a vivid image, memorable quotation or engaging anecdote.
- ❖ Use slides to enhance your message with vivid imagery and charts.

Leaving the "spice" out of PowerPoint presentations will invite yawns and rolled eyes. Don't make the mistake many women make of leaving the "spice of life" at the corporate front door.

Make It Sweet

Anoush ella. The Arabic proverb "Let it be sweet" applies to both cooking and life. Without a little sugar, the world would be a very dull place. Look at the pinched faces of any South Beach dieter the first three weeks of the diet. Instead of running away from the adage, "sugar and spice and everything nice," embrace it. In every woman, there lives a sweet, nice, spicy, lovely girl waiting to come out.

Let sweetness come into your workday, from fresh flowers on your desk to a cheerful greeting on your voice mail. Put a dollop of honey into your voice before you answer the phone. You'll be amazed at the results.

One expert receptionist taught herself to breathe two or three times before answering every call so could answer the company phone with a sweet voice. She was so good at bringing "sweet" into the workplace that the corporate trainer asked her to teach all the division employees in the company her techniques for answering the phone "sweetly."

Studies show that women who do not commit gender violation advance higher than those perceived to exhibit the more masculine traits of aggression, direct communication, and declaration. Women who master the art of requesting, collaborating, and complimenting advance quicker than those who are perceived to be "acting like men" (Babcock and Laschever, 2003).

A Pinch of Salt, a Dash of Hope

When delivering bad news, always couch your message with the promise of better things to come. Firsthand, I learned this lesson when I had to deliver news that sent several long-term employees dissolving into tears.

We had to close a division of about 500 employees at a Fortune 500 company for which I worked. Many employees in that division had worked in the semiconductor industry for 20 years. Many had done the same job repeatedly in those 20 years. So when we announced the closing of the division and massive job layoffs, it felt more like a tub of salt than a dash of hope. Fortunately, this corporation valued its talent pool and gave all its potentially laid-off employees six to nine months to find new jobs within the corporation, a luxury most companies do not offer.

Ironically, many fabrication operators and testers went on to new and more fulfilling careers and lives, moving their families out of the high-priced San Francisco Bay Area and in to the more affordable communities of Colorado Springs, Colorado; Roseville, California; and Corvallis, Oregon. They traded their half-a-million-dollar homes for $100K homes in areas with good public school districts. Some hardware engineers got fresh starts on their careers, mid-life, as software engineers with a company retraining program. Still other operators learned new computer skills that led them into higher-paying computer technician jobs. At the end of that year, 95 percent of the roughly 500 employees had been placed in new jobs or new careers within the company.

So now, whenever I have to convey hard news, I remember to limit the negative to a pinch and accentuate the positive with a full dash. Historically, every worse-case scenario, even dot.com company busts, has turned into a positive success story for me and those around me.

Love the Journey

When the president of a small, private liberal arts university in the Oakland hills greets new students every fall orientation, she always says the same thing: "Love the journey" (Nassif, 2005). Whether you are in the boardroom or bored, if you love the journey, you will enjoy a great experience.

Not every job is going to be your dream job. Some are downright rotten.

One Wells Fargo Bank vice president hated her two years at the call center in Concord, California, but loved the experience of learning every aspect of the bank's operation at the customer-facing level. That experience positioned her well for her corporate gig as trainer in business banking. She made the suburban outpost job tolerable by taking walks at noon and getting to know every aspect of the bank's consumer offerings. Now, back at the corporate headquarters in San Francisco, she knows more than most of her colleagues about the nitty-gritty of getting the job done.

Chef's Choice

Always remember, it's a choice. Your choice. Just as you orchestrate the meals that come out of your kitchen, you choose the direction you want to pursue. Whether a boom economy or a bust, your career is your own.

If you choose to stay in an organization, know exactly why you are doing so and focus on all the pluses of making that choice. Never blame anyone else for the choices you have elected to make. Remember, you always have a choice.

One couple, caught in the Silicon Valley downturn that followed the dot.com bust, had not worked for two years. Their marriage was suffering. Their spirits were sagging. The woman of the pair confessed to a deep-seated feeling of despair. However, after looking at the situation objectively, it was clear that the power couple with MBAs from prestigious universities and 10 years each of blue-chip corporate experience and a million-dollar home purchased 10 years ago, had many options. They could sell their home and live off the interest of their investment. They could move to Seattle, Austin, or the Tech Triangle in North Carolina or near the 128 corridor outside Boston. They could move in with her parents in Los Altos or his parents in

Hawaii and rent out the house for the mortgage payment and a positive cash flow. They didn't make any of those choices. They made an even better one. They drew on their prior stock savings, partnered with another couple in the same boat and purchased a thriving business from a retiring couple. All three couples thrived in the win-win choice that ensured fulfillment and financial rewards for all of them. So, dire as their circumstances appeared, they had many options and chose one that led them out of the dismal space they had sunk into during the bust.

It is your choice. As with any good chef, the more recipes in your cookbook, the more choices you give yourself for the wonderful meal of life.

Inside Jobs

Steve Jobs, founder of Apple Computers and Pixar, is one of the most remarkable CEOs in the Fortune 500. He dumped Disney when Pixar was not getting the returns he felt fair for creating one of the highest-grossing computer-generated animation films of all time, *Finding Nemo*. He then negotiated one of the biggest buyouts in history. Jobs, parlaying his $10 million investment into $7.4 billion, became the largest shareholder of the parent company, Disney, at 7 percent, a full 5 percent ahead of the next largest shareholder, Eisner. From the beginning, Jobs counseled that "the journey is the reward." No other Fortune 500 CEO has made that statement more real.

Unfortunately, most of you don't take this advice. Americans, who take an average of less than two weeks' vacation a year and give back an average of one week a year, wait until retirement to begin to travel or do the things they really enjoy doing. The sad fact is that, by retirement, many are too disabled, too lethargic, or too dispirited to begin to do what they love.

Whatever You Do

Wherever you go, whatever you do, savor the experience. Then you will always be happy. Because, as Ram Dass (1971) says, the only moment we have is now. Even after a debilitating stroke, Ram Dass managed to complete another book of Buddhist philosophy, *Still Here* (Dass, 2000), extolling the virtues of living in the moment.

Approach cooking and love with abandon. May you abandon yourself to savor the experience.

Exercises

1. List all the careers you've had so far. Next to each career, describe the talents and skills you've developed on your "cook's tour."

2. List all the ways you can "go somewhere you've never been before" this year and do as many of them as you can muster.

3. Identify all the training programs you might sign up for this year and sign up for as many as you can juggle with your work schedule.

4. Make a list under each heading: (1) Learn; (2) Earn; (3) Return. Next to each category, list five ways you've managed through each of the three "seasons" of your life's repeating cycles.

5. List five ways you can be more yourself at your job. Select one and do it for eight weeks. Then, select another, and do that for eight weeks. (It takes eight weeks to form a habit.)

6. Visualize your next career move. Do the one hard thing—budgets, international assignments, management—that will get you to your next level.

7. Name your deepest desire. Identify the time you have available to pursue that passion. If your job interferes with the pursuit of your passion, consider taking time off to pursue your passion.

8. Find books of humor, positive quotations, and anecdotes and keep them at your desk. Add one new story, joke, or quotation to each of your PowerPoint presentations.

9. Learn one new software program—Snap, Excel, Adobe Photoshop—that will enhance the visuals in your corporate presentations.

10. List all the ways you could be sweeter to yourself, your colleagues, and your boss. Do at least one for each audience a week.

11. Prepare your next "bad news" announcement with a positive dash of hope. Read Marianne Williamson or Louise Hay to uncover how you can turn bad news into good.

12. List all the areas of your life that matter. Next to each area, describe the choice you made and at what

juncture you chose it to be where you are as a way of recognizing both your choices and the consequences of those choices.

13.   Describe your ideal day. Now, describe your real day. See how you can make it more congruent so that you can "love the journey."

14.   List all the things you love about your job. If the list is fewer than five, find another job.

15.   Find a technique—meditation, yoga, t'ai chi—that helps you develop the discipline required to be in the moment. As you practice these disciplines, extend the experience of being here now to all that you do.

16.   Take a class in cooking and, while in the class, discipline yourself to be fully present, forgetting any worries, as you learn a new skill that can help you savor life's experiences.

Chapter 10

Power up, power down, power through.

The Athlete

*In our day, when a pitcher got into trouble in a game,
instead of taking him out, our manager would leave
him in and tell him to pitch his way out of trouble.*

~ Cy Young
baseball pitching great

Olympic Moment

Everyone has the potential to have an Olympic moment.
It is the moment of truth when all the discipline and practice
of all the years of your training come to bear on a single moment
when you can win or lose the game. Nowhere was this more
evident than when the aging U.S. soccer team faced the Brazil
team in the 2004 Olympics in Athens. Fighting for gold, the
score was tied in regulation. Going to overtime, Kristi Lilly
headed the ball to the next generation soccer teammate who
banged it in for the gold. The U.S. women won 2 to 1 against

one of the world soccer powerhouses, with six mid-30-year-olds, dinosaurs in Olympic sports. Mia Hamm, Brandi Chastain, Kristi Lilly, Julie Foudy, Briana Scurry, and Joy Fawcett said goodbye to the sport they had made popular in the United States in the span of a single lifetime.

These women took the game of soccer from near oblivion to the front of the sports pages across America. They built a professional women's soccer league and saw it die before their prime.

Through it all, the U.S. women's soccer team's mature six players powered up, powered down, and powered through an unprecedented gold medal win over the Chinese in 1996 in Los Angeles, becoming the first American team ever to win gold in the sport. Then they suffered a heartbreaking loss to Norway, 3-2, settling for silver in 2000 in Sydney, and made an incredible comeback to win gold again in 2004.

This amid murmurs in the media that the women soccer athletes over 30 were "over the hill." The lesson of the 2004 U.S. women's soccer team's senior players is a lesson every successful athlete has learned: You win some and you lose some, but, no matter what, you keep on keepin' on.

Lessons of the Dot.Com Bust

Sports, especially since Title IX and the requirement that colleges and universities offer equal opportunity, including equal numbers of scholarships and women's sports teams, are great preparation for professional life. You must be resilient not only in an athletic contest but in your work life as well.

During the high-tech boom of the 80s and 90s, women professionals including Meg Whitman, CEO of eBay; Carly Fiorina, former CEO of Hewlett-Packard; Stephanie DiMarco,

CEO of Advent Software; and Carol Bartz, executive chairman of the board and former CEO of Autodesk rose to the top of their fields. When the bust came in 2000, many high-tech professionals, women and men alike, left the field for good. In three years, from 2000 to 2003, the San Francisco Bay Area, including hardest-hit Silicon Valley, lost half of all the jobs lost in the U.S. during that period.

The dot.com bust taught the bitter lesson that nothing lasts forever. All that glitters is not gold. Easy wins make for easy losses. Quick money vanishes just as quickly as it appears.

So what does a successful corporate professional do?

As every world-class athlete knows, there are no guarantees in the board game of life. Four years of disciplined training and dedicated effort don't always yield a gold medal. The British marathon runner favored to win the 2004 Olympic race collapsed on the run up one more Athens hill in 100-degree heat without even finishing the race she'd trained for her whole life. Jackie Joyner Kersee, world champion, did not even qualify for the Athens 2004 Olympics. Pole vaulter Stacy Dragila missed all three of her easily cleared prior jumps in the final trials to leave the field without a gold medal.

But veteran swimmer Jenny Thompson became the most decorated American athlete with 12 total medals in a lifetime despite her mother's death from cancer the year before. She's now retired to pursue her medical degree full-time. And Natalie Coughlin, a Cal-Berkeley graduate, took gold in the 100-meter backstroke, 100-meter freestyle, 4x100-meter medley relay, and 4x200-meter freestyle relay. Out of nowhere, Joanna Hayes took gold in the 100-meter hurdles, the only American woman to take gold in the usually American-dominant track and field events.

Win or lose, there are five things world-class athletes can teach women professionals:

1. Go for it!
2. Always do your best.

3. Relentlessly train for success.
4. Play to your strengths.
5. Win or lose, enjoy the game.

No Pain, No Gain

If you stay in your safe job, chances are it will not remain safe or, even if it does, you will become bored with it.

My sister has counted the 119 days to retirement remaining in her 32 years in government. The problem is, now that she is just days away from retirement, she has discovered that what she thought was sufficient monthly income from her retirement fund is no longer enough to live on and she must add five years or 1,825 days to the countdown. The sad fact is, she's steadily lost years of her life's energy doing a safe job she's hated for an oppressive and overbearing employer. Her safety net has become her prison door.

Don't avoid a challenge just because it's tough. It is often the challenges of your career that enliven you. Like steel forged in fire, you are strengthened by the flames of adventure. On your career path, it is always true, "no pain, no gain." The greatest rewards go to the greatest risk takers. That's why salespeople, in *Fortune* magazine study after study, make more, on average, than any other job category, including executive positions. The only job area of greater reward is entrepreneur and, as you all know, that also carries the greatest risk.

Train, Train, and Train Some More

Jerry Rice, the standout former wide receiver in the National Football League, exemplified the discipline of great athletes. He played past age 40. After a sun-drenching workout, when all the players return to the locker room for a refreshing shower, Jerry returned to the field to run up and down the bleachers. He wanted to ensure that he was in the best physical condition of any player on the field. And, now, on *Dancing With the Stars*, Rice displays a willingness to learn a brand-new sport—ballroom dancing. He even took ballet lessons for the first time to perfect his posture and his extension.

As a corporate athlete, you want to prove yourself a long-distance runner. The best way to ensure the longevity of your career, despite downsizing and outsourcing overseas, is to train better than anyone else in your field.

Take advantage of all the in-house training courses. Most women claim that they don't have time to go to training. If you want your company to value you, value yourself. One of the best uses of your time is continuous learning on the job. Great companies offer great training opportunities, everything from training based on Stephen Covey's *Seven Habits of Highly Effective People* to Jim Collins *Good to Great* to Spencer Johnson's *The Present*.

Often, the best training is delivered by professional trainers off-site. One of the most useful classes I ever attended was a week-long executive presentations class taught by professional public speakers to San Francisco Bay Area executives. The course demanded that we create impromptu, informative, extemporaneous, dramatic, and persuasive speeches. We were videotaped and critiqued. Following each critique, we had to change our speeches to incorporate the coaches' suggestions. Our last speeches were delivered to a hostile audience. We were required to field angry, confrontational questions and overcome heckling from the audience. I learned more in a week about public speaking than I had learned in a lifetime of speech classes, tournaments, and forensics training.

Don't overlook local colleges and universities. Targeted programs of continuing education can lead to certification in Microsoft customer engineering or human resources management. Executive leadership certificate and executive MBA programs can extend your network of high-powered contacts, as well as expand your knowledge of business management.

The top staff recruiting firm in the country, Haldane Associates, now estimates that training is one of the top three drivers of all job choice decisions.

Portfolio Worker

The *Harvard Business Review* was the first and, by no means the last, to identify the phenomenon of the "portfolio worker" (*www.cefe.org/acve*). No longer guaranteed a job for life, company loyalty has taken a back seat to career loyalty. Career experts estimate that the average number of careers, not merely jobs, which most Americans will have is at least five in a lifetime. Not only will you change jobs as frequently as every two to five years, but you will change careers nearly as often, as well. Because job security is fast becoming elusive to all but a few civil service and federal government workers, your best insurance against job loss in a global economy is to build up your portfolio of skills, project successes, and work samples.

No longer the purview of advertising copywriters and graphic designers, who have long understood the value of creating and updating a book of work samples to demonstrate creativity, brilliant conceptual design, and outstanding business results, all professionals should be prepared to demonstrate their value to a prospective or current employer.

Portfolio workers are so called because they build and enhance a portfolio of skills during every job that they take to the next job. Like all expatriates, they learn to develop a suite of intellectual, business, creative talents, and skills that can literally be packed in a suitcase on a moment's notice. While today's workers are not running for their lives, it often feels that way to some who have weathered four, five, and 10 layoffs in as many years as a result of swift direction changes and globalization.

The Stanford Engineering Department estimates that 90 percent of what engineers learn today will be obsolete in five years (diPaolo, 2001). This pace of change affects other careers, too. So if you're not acquiring new skills, you are not just standing still. You're losing ground.

Go the Extra Mile

Mike Phelps, winner of eight medals, six gold and two bronze, in the 2004 Olympics, swims seven miles. (That's 252 laps every day!) So, the next time you're in the pool and your one-mile workout of 36 laps seems too long, keep swimming.

As with physical excellence, professional excellence results from a consistent willingness to "go the extra mile."

The best coaches inspire, not require, the extra mile. I learned this lesson loud and clear one foggy morning when the sound of slapping water awoke me in my tent. I went down to the river at sunrise to see several black-capped women swimming the first leg of the "Half-Vineman Race," a 1.2-mile Russian River swim, 56-mile bike ride, and 13.2-mile run for the annual wine country marathon race. A woman on the banks yelled out, "You got it! Great job! Keep going! You can do it!" And with each cheer, the swimmers gave it another go, even when the current stymied them or a buoy bonked them on the head.

Nordstrom has built its business on this principle. Service extends beyond the parking lot. One salesperson hand-delivered a dress to a customer who needed it for that evening.

Recession-proof Mercedes-Benz continues to thrive. Mileage on used vehicles is guaranteed to 100,000 miles or five years. Mercedes believes in the gold standard of quality of customer service and exceeds every benchmark, including sustained value. The Mercedes-Benz is one of the few cars that appreciates in value, rather than depreciates, the moment you drive it off the lot.

Do you want your customer service to resemble a mass-market Costco or a high-end Nordstrom? Do you want the quality of your work to reflect the lowest-end Kia or the highest-end Mercedes-Benz? If you do Mercedes-Benz work with Nordstrom-level customer service consistently, you'll always be in high demand.

"Know When to Fold 'Em"

Staying in a dead-end job is soul-killing. Digging into a massive bureaucracy, year in and year out, can result in not only heartburn, but also heart attack. If, on the other hand, your job constantly requires insane hours, weekends, overnight travel, and killer schedules, then it's time to re-evaluate.

The brilliant woman professional is not afraid to quit while she's ahead or leave before the job leaves her bedraggled and depleted.

Fear keeps many smart women in overworked and undervalued situations. Have the faith in your own gut instincts to leave positions that encroach upon your personal and family time. Have the self-confidence to leave jobs that deplete your spirit. Whether or not you have an alternative, sometimes you must quit while you're ahead.

Power Down

Serena Williams understands the short life cycle of a pro tennis player. The world-class athlete has already prepared for her exit at the young age of 23. Securing one of the largest endorsement contracts of any woman athlete in history, Serena's $55 million-dollar, five-year contract with Nike sets her up for a lifetime of financial security. While winning a Grand Slam, Serena has devoted many hours to creating a hip, crossover line of women's sportswear. She models her own designs at Wimbledon, the Australian Open, and the U.S. Open. She even is set to appear in films before she tries to launch a full-blown acting career in Hollywood. Her sister, Venus, just came back from crushing injuries and personal tragedy to overwhelm Lindsay Davenport at Wimbledon in 2005. The Williams sisters are criticized for playing less than a full schedule on the tennis tour, but they have already learned what many world-class athletes fail to see: It is important to know how and when to "power down" in your career. Their light schedule and other interests have actually positioned them for success beyond tennis. And paved the way for huge Nike endorsements for up-and-comers Maria Sharapova in tennis and Michelle Wie in golf.

Even if you're at the top of your game, as a top saleswoman, top engineer, or top manager, know that every profession has a limited shelf life. Sales, for most women, peaks at age 45 or younger. After 45, many women lose the allure that moves most sales forward. There are exceptions in certain fields and with individual women, but, for the most part, selling the sizzle is hard to do after age 45. Most managers are seen as past tense after age 55. Even male corporate executives are urged to retire by age 60. More than half the new hires at Hewlett-Packard are college recruits because, in the fast-paced world of R&D

engineering, young college students are seen to have the advantage. So if you find yourself nearing the end-of-life age benchmark of your career, consider your power-down options.

For some, it means buying down in a rural or smaller community with a lower cost of living. For others, it means going back to school to become an educator, counselor, or therapist. Some fields, such as ministry, writing, education, counseling, therapy, real estate, financial planning, insurance sales, and college teaching, regard maturity a plus. In fields where wisdom and experience are valued, age is an asset. So consider preparing yourself to wind down from high-powered corporate jobs and enter into more low-key, flexible, life-enriching fields.

Power Through

You may have to work until you're 70. That's not going to be so unusual when you consider that the average life expectancy for U.S. women today is 79.9 (CDC, 2005). There are so many women living into their 90s that if you check the birthday section of your local Hallmark store, you'll find several cards in the age-90 category. That was unheard of until recently. Just 10 years ago, most retirement plans were geared to a shorter life expectancy, so the money needed to retire at 60 is much greater for someone who lives 30 more years than for someone who only lives 10 more years.

With half of marriages ending in divorce, women wind up the biggest losers (Hochschild, 1989, 2003). Most women lose 66 percent of their earnings in a divorce, while most men double their income following a split.

Suze Orman, author of *9 Steps to Financial Freedom* (Orman, 2000) and cable television talk show host, urges women to "know your money." At every women's conference she addresses, Suze asks, "How many of you don't have a separate credit card or checking account in your name only?" Often, a good 20 percent of the women in the audience raise their hands. Then Orman points out all the pitfalls of leaving the money matters to your husband.

According to Orman, more women wind up impoverished than men due to three primary reasons:

1. Women live longer than men.
2. Women make less money than men.
3. Women rarely know how to manage money well.

One of the best insurance policies against poverty in old age is to know and learn to manage your money.

Then, when the downturns come or the layoffs hit, you, unlike most American women, will be prepared to weather the bad economy for a year if you have saved a year's salary.

No matter what the adversity, your willingness to power through tough situations will sustain you. As the Kaiser ad campaign "Thrive" admonishes: Good health is not one big choice, but all the little decisions you make every day.

Here are everyday choices that will help you power through:

1. Practice extreme self-care:
   - ❖ Eat nutritiously.
   - ❖ Get enough sleep.
   - ❖ Exercise regularly.
   - ❖ Build and nurture a community of friends.
   - ❖ Put a positive spin on events.
   - ❖ Take one positive action toward your big goals daily.
   - ❖ When discouraged or upset, talk it out with a trusted friend, minister, colleague, or relative.

2.   Write out your goals in measurable terms and monitor your progress monthly.

3.   When you fail, quickly analyze what you have learned from the failure, and apply the learning to the next similar situation.

4.   Read something inspirational, if only for 10 minutes, every day.

Whether laid off or divorced, whether retiring early or not retiring at all, the most enduring strength you have to rely on is yourself, your flexibility, your grace, your talents, your confidence, and your attitude.

The biggest obstacle you will ever face is your own mental attitude.

When in Doubt, Row

Debra Veal, MBE, MA, entered the Trans-Atlantic boat race with her husband, a 6-foot 5-inch experienced oarsman. He abandoned the boat after developing an uncontrollable fear. The British BBC broadcaster continued on alone, despite her inexperience and 5-foot 5-inch stature. The one message she taped onto the mirror of the galley of the ship was "Choose Your Attitude," and every day, she powered through fears, doubts, seasickness, storms, and drifts backward.

That woman in her mid-20s recognized that mental attitude is a choice. You cannot choose your circumstances, or even affect them necessarily, but you can choose your response.

The best response to mounting difficulties, like the 25-foot swells or a company-wide round of layoffs, is to put your oar in the sea and row. Row even when you can't see what's up ahead. Row even if you don't get anywhere, as Debra did when, some days, she realized she had continually gone backward due to heavy winds and strong currents.

As long as you take some positive action, no matter how hard your circumstances, you eventually will succeed in business, probably; in life, for sure.

Power Up, Power Down, Power Through

When starting a new job, a new career, or a new business, you have to gear up for success. You have to put in extra hours and put forth extra effort.

When coming to the end of a big run or a shift in priorities, you need to power down. Whether to raise a child, go back to school, or switch careers, you may have to slow down and change direction.

You're more than your cute figure or power suit. It's the you inside the aerobics outfit that counts.

Sometimes, when circumstances get really rough, you lose a job, you suffer a death or illness in the family, you divorce, or you're in an extended financial downturn at your company, getting through is all you need to do. Every athlete who goes down in the record books or lands in the Hall of Fame has learned to power through a hitting slump, a scoring drought, an injury layoff. The final discipline every athlete must master is to power through. Nicole Powell, a Stanford women's basketball player and now WNBA player, overcame a serious back injury to become a two-time All American. Swimmer Natalie Coughlin overcame shoulder injury to become an Olympic gold medal winner. Martina Navratilova overcame knee surgery and pulled endorsements resulting from her coming out as a lesbian to become one of the all-time greatest women tennis champions and longest-running professional doubles players at age 45. Whether you have been an Olympic athlete or just rock at your local jazz aerobics class, know that you have the ability to power up when starting anything new, power down when circumstances change, and power through when the going gets tough. As the great Notre Dame football coach Knute Rockne said, "When the going gets tough, the tough get going. Win this one for the Gipper."

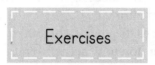

Exercises

1. Select a challenging athletic feat and master all the practice required to complete the challenge. Examples:
    ❖ Marathon
    ❖ Triathlon
    ❖ Breast cancer or AIDS Walkathon
    ❖ Dance performance

2. Select a workout goal and determine a positive daily action required to reach the goal. Map out steps for eight weeks, because it takes eight weeks to form a habit.

3. List 10 careers you'd consider pursuing. Pick one and map out a strategy for getting there.

4. List 10 jobs you'd love to have. Pick one and create a plan for securing the new job within a year.

5. Write down all your skills with money. Now, write down all your weaknesses. Pick one area of weakness and create a plan to overcome that weakness.

6. Identify five financial planners in your area. Check references of all five. Pick one to help create a financial plan for yourself.

7. Find out about all the self-care classes your health insurance carrier offers. Pick at least one a year to complete.

8. Hire a fitness trainer, coach, or weight-loss counselor. Set a health goal for the year and get the help to make it happen.

9. Name three areas you'd like to have more skill in for your current job. Pick one and take a class, a training course, or a workshop on that area.

10. List the 20 percent aspects of your job that create 80 percent of the value. Spend 80 percent of each workday on those 20 percent.

11. Identify customer service standards in your business and give yourself a ranking of 10 to 100, 100 being the best. For any ranking less than 100, name three things you could easily do to improve your score and do them.

12. Identify quality standards for your product or service and give yourself a ranking of 10 to 100. For any ranking less than 100, name three things you could easily do to improve your score and do them.

13. If you're in a bad situation, name five things you could do every week to pave the way out of that situation and do them.

14. Periodically, list the five most important goals and values in your life (these may shift). Make sure that 90 percent of your time is spent on those top five. If

your job is interfering with accomplishing those top five, consider your alternatives.

15. Develop your own succession plan. If you're a top salesperson, engineer, or manager, decide when you plan to call it quits and what you plan to do with the rest of your life.

Chapter 11

Do your Dharma.

The Soul Sister

If you always do what interests you,
at least one person is pleased.

~ Katharine Hepburn
award-winning actress

Do What You Love

Caryn Elaine Johnson knew what she wanted to be for as long as she could remember. She spent the first years of her life in a public housing project in Chelsea. She made her performing debut at age eight with the Helena Rubenstein Children's Theatre at the Hudson Guild in Manhattan. But she dropped out of high school and got hooked on heroin. Despite several setbacks, she landed jobs in the choruses of the Broadway hits *Hair, Jesus Christ Superstar,* and *Pippin.*

At 33, she was discovered by director Mike Nichols and in 1984, Nichols presented her on Broadway in a one-woman show of her own creation. Her show was a smash hit, bringing her to the attention of Steven Spielberg who cast her in the leading film role in Alice Walker's Pulitzer Prize-winning novel, *The Color Purple*. Subsequently, her performance in *Ghost* won her an Academy Award and a Golden Globe Award for Best Supporting Actress. In the 1990s, Whoopi Goldberg, also known as Caryn Johnson, was cast in more films than just about any other actor *(www.imdb.com)*.

When she first told her mother she wanted to be an actor, her mother's only advice was, "It may be tough, but what isn't?"

So remember, whatever the obstacles, you came here with your own unique set of talents and strengths. You have a "work" to fulfill. Know that nothing worth doing is easy and that it's going to be tough, anyway, so it might as well be tough achieving what your soul came here to do.

Do What You Love Whether the Money Follows or Not

No matter what happens to you, you always have yourself. If you follow your heart's path, you will always find happiness, if not money. Paradoxically, if you do what you love, you're usually good at it and often attract abundance in the service of doing what you enjoy most.

Take a writer, for example. A real writer must write, whether paid or not. A writer writes because she must. Words are the food of her life and sentences are the threads by which she weaves the tapestry of her life.

Even Nobel Prize winners for literature generally write in modest circumstances. The $1.3 million is a surprise to most writers toiling in relative obscurity. The winner of the 2004 Nobel Prize for Literature, Austrian Elfriede Jelinek, at 57, was one of the youngest writers to win the prize. She did not want to leave her private life even to accept the award in Stockholm and asked not to attend.

Most writers write for years before they are recognized or financially rewarded. ZZ Packer, author of *Drinking Coffee Elsewhere* (Packer, 2003), has been working for five years on a novel. Her agent, a representative for two Pulitzer Prize–winning authors, says it took both authors 10 years to write their novels. So writers keep writing because writing is what defines them. Writing saves them when times are tough and expands them even further when times are good.

Writers take only a pen and paper with them anywhere. Their tools are simple and their needs are small. A laptop or PC can bring a finishing touch to a manuscript, but, if imprisoned, a pad of paper and pen suffice to comfort them. Anwar Sadat, former Egyptian President and winner of the Nobel Peace Prize along with Israeli Prime Minister Menachem Begin, was jailed and confined to solitary for two years; he wrote essays in his mind to keep his sanity during confinement.

So you must find out what you love to do. What would you do if no one paid you or recognized your work? When you find out what that is for you, do it. Doing what you love brings more happiness, without the dependence on anyone else, than almost anything else in the world can bring you. When Humphrey Bogart died, his wife (Lauren Bacall) maintained that she got through by acting, work she adored almost as much as she had adored him.

What If I Don't Know What I Love to Do?

Many of you don't know what you want to be when you grow up. That's because, like most women, you have spent your life taking care of everyone else's needs. Mary Oliver, Pulitzer Prize–winning poet, asks, "Tell me, what is it you plan to do with your one wild and precious life?" Your most important mission in life is discovering who you are and what you came here to contribute.

While being a mom is a very noble profession, it is not enough. Once your children grow up, then what? And being a wife is not enough, either, because devoting yourself to your husband or partner's goals doesn't leave you with enough of a sense of your separate self to make you an intriguing and magnetic partner.

The best way to find out what you love is to imagine what you would do if you had no financial or familial constraints. Usually, the first thing that comes to your mind is the most accurate.

An expert in career counseling, Dr. Barbara Sher, herself a single mother turned author and television personality, suggests that you uncover your passion and pursue it. Pursue it part time, if you must, but pursue your dreams with fervor. Her books and videotapes, including *Wishcraft* (Sher, 1983) and *How To Create Your Second Life After 40* (Sher, 1998), can help you, step by step, find out what your passion is and how to actualize your dreams.

Start Small

You cannot fail if you start small.

If you think you want to be an artist, take a drawing class at the local adult education, community college, or university extension programs. If you think you'd like to own a gardening store, work part time at one and see if you really like the day-to-day responsibilities of running such a store. If you think you want to teach, begin by teaching Sunday school at your local church or charitable giving courses at your synagogue. If you'd like to become a caterer, start by catering a relative's baby shower, birthday party, or wedding. Do it for free as a test case.

One couple, eager to start a French bed-and-breakfast tour business, hosted their French families for a week where they tested all the recipes, tours, and timing. The families got a vacation in the South of France and their tour guides, French Escapade, worked out the details of their business at no cost to customer satisfaction.

Kiss a Lot of Frogs

As with finding the right company for you, you may have to kiss a lot of frogs before you find the handsome prince of a career.

In the Buddhist sense, finding your dharma means finding the work your soul came here to do. So finding one's dharma is no small task.

Given the current realities of American work, you will most likely have five careers in a lifetime—not just five jobs, but five distinct careers. And they may not always be with companies that value and promote you.

Nely Galán, born in Cuba, moved with her family to New Jersey when she was two. By the time she was a young adult, she knew what she wanted to do and set about doing it, working for one of the toughest television producers in New York City. After years of long hours and dedication, she was passed over for an executive position. In a heated exchange, the company owner gave her the best advice of her career: "If you want to make the decisions, start your own company!" She wasn't quite ready for that, but she never forgot that bittersweet moment when she left her first production company to become president of entertainment at one of the largest Spanish-language network television stations, Telemundo. Today, Galán has her own piece of advice: Whatever you do, "always be the pink couch" (*Galan*, 2003). What she means is take your unique differentiator and emphasize, rather than diminish, it. Nely Galán did just that when she started Galan Entertainment, becoming one of "the most powerful young executives in Hollywood," according to *The New York Times*. Now, she shares with you just how you can transform yourself from the ugly duckling you might feel you are to the beautiful swan within in her latest role as life coach on the Fox–TV hit show, *The Swan*.

It may take a long time before you discover your life's work, and once you discover it, it may take a while before you can pursue that work full time. Not to worry. Each experience expands you and offers you a chance to grow. Dharma, being bigger than any career, encapsulates a vision for life. You can use all the experiences of every one of those careers on the way to finding your soul's work.

In fact, be driven by courage. Try everything, at least once, that strikes your fancy. Follow your interests, even when you don't know where they will lead you. A dance class can make you a new friend. A Spanish class can improve your rapport with your Latino line staff. A meditation class can become the backdrop of a stress relief workshop you run. You never know where the road will lead you. If you're following your heart, you're sure to arrive at your dharma.

Just Do It (Nike)

So many of you think and think, dream and analyze, but never do.

I know. I'm just like you. For years, I've been dreaming of having property in the wine country of Sonoma county. In fact, I've been thinking about it for nearly 20 years. Finally, I've met with a realtor and gotten on an e-mail distribution that sends me new property listings daily. I've met with a financial planner to determine exactly what I need to do to make my dream a reality. That's just one example of hoping and wishing and praying that my dream would come true with no real action plan to make it true. Whatever you're dreaming of, just do it.

If you want to act, audition for a play. If you want to play the piano, take piano lessons. If you want to run a marathon, sign up for the annual Leukemia Marathon run for free practices and coaching and make your first marathon count for something beyond yourself. In fact, the main characteristic of doing your dharma is that it will be work that benefits others. It will be something that encompasses a big idea, one that transcends both time and space. Whatever you come up with, quit thinking about it and begin doing it.

Follow Your Passion

Meg Whitman, one of Fortune 500's most influential women CEOs, told the Princeton University Class of 2002 to "always love what you do." Meg, as she is known in the eBay "community," urged graduates to do more than just that, and led by example with a $30 million Whitman family gift to Princeton for the construction of Whitman College, a new experiential and social educational model. A member of the Steering Committee for the Women in Leadership Initiative, Whitman encourages all alumnæ to volunteer and participate in philanthropy in their respective communities. She knows what eludes many self-serving executives: Giving back is as fulfilling as giving your all to your passion.

How to Find Meaning in Your Work

"Let's paint something immortal," said the bald-headed seven-year-old with the IVs stuck in her tiny arm. From the hospital bed at the top of Parnassus Street in San Francisco, the Chinese-American girl with inoperable lymphoma had told her teacher what all the adults caring for her were afraid to admit. In one sentence, she articulated the desire in all of us for meaning in our lives—to count, to matter, to make a difference to someone sometime forever. She knew she was dying, though no one had said it. She wanted to do more than her ABCs and multiplication tables before she took her last breath. With blue eyes watering, her teacher fought to keep the tears from rolling down her cheeks when she heard what the girl had said. The teacher pulled out a roll of white paper and reached into her beat-up leather briefcase for eight colored markers. As if by magic, the little girl's eyes glistened as she moved the paint markers onto the page, filling the blankness with her own stamp of immortality. What did she paint? An empress floating on a silk pillow, the sun rising through gilded pagodas behind her like faith.

You and I are not different from that little girl. We may have more years to live. Nevertheless, we want the same thing, to "paint something immortal." That painting is not going to be the ABCs of your jobs or the budget spreadsheets of your title-confined positions; it's going to be something more.

Alan Briskin, in *The Stirring of Soul in the Workplace* (1996), says, "The challenge to meaning should not be underestimated…meaning cannot come from corporate mission statements; it is sought through dialogue and reflection, through the courage to ask troubling questions and a willingness to face the consequences of our collective and individual actions."

To find meaning in a corporation is an inside job. First, you must discover meaning in work you love. How will you recognize work you love? You'll lose track of time. You'll have lots of energy when you do it. You'll be naturally good at it. Obstacles won't phase you. You'll be singularly happy whether or not anyone recognizes what you've done. This doing of work you love, even within the confines of a Fortune 500 company, will bring you meaning.

Like Falling in Love

In fact, it is like falling in love. You will throw caution to the wind to pursue the object of your affections. You will endure sleepless nights and days with little food. You will ignore every friend to rest with your beloved. And who is this magnificent love? It is right within your grasp. It is, in fact, beating in your heart this very moment. It is your soul's purpose, the work you were meant to do.

When you fall in love with your work, you have found a love that lasts forever. Be forewarned, you may end up having to give up every old notion of yourself. And for that high roll of the dice, you risk finding your joy, your essence, the meaning in your life. You will join with that little girl and, with the work of your life, paint something immortal.

One Love That Won't Desert You

Lovers come and go. Children grow up and move out. Money comes and goes. Opportunities materialize and evaporate. But one thing remains constant. If you love your work, you always have access to that regenerating life force within you. You are always centered. Buffered against the storms of the world's shifting fortunes, you have a power deep within that you can call upon regardless of external circumstances.

How to Find Work You Love in a Corporation

One woman had been ousted from the world of mortgage banking when the commercial building market dried up. After a bitter divorce that left her a single parent with two small boys to raise and an enormous mortgage to pay without alimony and very little child support, she had spent her entire work life in banking. At 58, she decided to pursue what she loved, and it turned out to be golf and tennis. How does a 58-year-old make a living in a young white man's sport? She pursued her passion right into a management position at one of the world's top golf courses, Pebble Beach. My friend plays golf and teaches top executive women in America how to use golf to succeed in business. She was laid off from the golf job at 62 and found a position with a mortgage lender through her golf connections. At 65, she was tapped to run one of the fastest-growing home mortgage offices with one of the largest lenders in the San Francisco Bay Area. Finding the company chauvinistic and limiting, she retired early to, you guessed it, play golf in La Quinta, California.

Another colleague loves gardening. She took her horticultural degree from Massey University in New Zealand and came to America to work for one of the largest landscape maintenance firms in the country. While much of her job as an operations manager involved people and budget management, she still hoisted ficus plants, selected white orchids for Nordstrom (one of her premier accounts) and replanted poinsettias when her technicians were out sick. If the accounts payable department got her down, she just hopped in her company Ford Explorer and headed for the Half Moon Bay Nurseryman's Exchange for a review of the potted primroses. She specialized in ornamentals, flowers that make the workplace a better place. At home, her hands were always in the dirt and her garden resembled an English countryside. Her work was her passion. In 2005, her division was bought by a conglomerate. Two months later, she secured a promotion at her former company in a new and expanded role as operations manager of a $4 million exterior plant business.

Another corporate professional married her love of Web design and instruction to become a corporate trainer at Autodesk. In her management role, she not only designed training modules, but also traveled all over the world. As a native of the Philippines, she gained opportunities through this corporate job far beyond the reach of her island upbringing.

Whether it's writing, building, treating, litigating, researching, selling, designing, teaching, managing, or creating new things, if you love doing it, you'll be both good at it and always have that talent and passion to call on regardless of the vicissitudes of life.

It is a kind of immortality to create an award-winning, memorable advertising campaign. In a pæan to eternity, software engineers design themselves into the brain of the computer. Using mathematical models, business systems gurus project futures of bank services and products into the next millennium.

There is no measure on loving what you do. It brings pleasure and joy without effort. It is natural and easy and energizing and enlivening. Even if there are obstacles, those challenges when engaged in doing what you love merely fuel even greater achievement.

It is worth every dark night of the soul, every shattered beginning, or painful ending to arrive at an awareness of who you really are and what you came here to do.

You may have to grind out budgets, author tedious reports, fill out redundant forms, or sit in endless meetings with boring, pontificating bosses before you discover work you love. But, like any love, the rewards for searching are great and constant when you finally find yourself doing work you love with people who share your vision in an environment that brings you light and joy.

How Do I Find the Love of My Life?

How It Won't Happen

Like the wallflower who wants to meet her soul mate, but doesn't ever want to go out, doesn't have the courage to call anyone, never wants to attend parties, take classes, join groups, or begin hobbies that might offer her opportunities to meet prospective partners, you cannot expect to find work that you deeply love by doing nothing or by continuing to do the same old thing over and over again.

How It Will Happen

It may seem obvious, but you may not be doing the easiest, most accessible thing you can do to find work you love. Begin by associating with people who are pursuing work you think you might love: gardeners, scientists, doctors, professors, engineers, lawyers, teachers, artists, writers, firefighters, criminologists, actors, advertising moguls, sales executives, ministers, politicians, musicians, contractors, entrepreneurs.

"Like Attracts Like"

There is an old metaphysical saying that I've found true in my life: "Like attracts like" (Ponder, 1966).

As you "hang out" with people of like interests, you will realize in your body how you feel when you're around them. Your breathing will deepen. Your muscles will relax. You'll laugh from the diaphragm. You'll be engaged. You'll feel energized. The experience of being around people you resonate with will resonate in your body.

For example, in my 20 years in high technology, I always enjoyed being around the graphic designers and writers in marketing departments. I always enjoyed good trainers. I found salespeople to be human, interested, and fun. Finally, I really liked the entrepreneurs, whether they were technical geniuses, marketing mavens, or e-commerce pioneers. I loved the contact with executives from around the world. Whether entrepreneurs or global executives, the thinking of these high-powered people was often irregular, original, refreshing, and broad.

As I associated with creative types in corporations, I found my meetings with the graphic designers, writers, video producers, and Web content developers to be fun, energizing, and absorbing. My collaborations with writers and my own copywriting gave me a sense of fulfillment. This was in stark contrast to the redundant staff operations meetings that left me bored and irritated. Or the remakes of budget forecasts that felt tedious. Going on sales calls with account managers from all over the world was a Zen practice. One had to stay present "in the moment" of every sales engagement, for a deal could be won or lost that instantly. Listening and forcing my mind into the day-tight compartment of a customer briefing was both demanding and rewarding. Presenting to a room of Chinese telecommunications government officials and executives with a translator was the ultimate challenge for all my teaching and public speaking skills. When they said to the translator, "She could be a politician," and asked to meet with our sales reps in Beijing, it was worth the stuttered flow back and forth to the translator and every ounce of body language reading skills I had learned in my earlier career as a psychodrama co-facilitator in a mental health center. Finally, entrepreneurs inspired and excited me. Their long vision and unusual thinking validated the often-lonely position I found myself in as a right-brain thinker in a left-brain world. This explains how I ended up a writer, professor, and entrepreneur—guilt by association, really.

"Hey Sister, Soul Sister, Go Sister!" ("Lady Marmalade," Crew and Nolan, 1997)

Go for it. Not just the next rung on the corporate ladder, but the real work you came here to pursue. When you do your dharma, doors will open. Most of all, you'll always be happy.

Exercises

1. Make a list of 10 passions. Next to each one, write the last time you did them. If you haven't done one in a long time and it's still a passion, circle it and make a plan to do it this month.

2. Divide a sheet of paper into two columns. In one column are the "likes" and in the other column are the "dislikes" about your job. See if you can incorporate a greater (25 percent or more) percentage of the "likes" into your existing job.

3. Make a list of classes you've always wanted to take. Circle the most exciting one. Get a copy of your local adult education, community college, or university extension catalog and take the class you're most interested in next semester.

4. On your list of passions, figure out a way to "hang out" with more of the people doing your interests. If you like rock climbing, for example, join the rock-climbing group of the Sierra Club. If you want to do more skiing, sign up for your company's or alumni's ski club.

5. On your list of passions, is there one that you would like personal tutoring in? Ballroom dancing? Flute lessons? Weight training? Pick one and hire a private tutor for eight sessions. (Remember, it takes eight weeks to form a habit.) Tara Van DerVeer, Stanford women's basketball coach, always wanted to play piano. So in the 2001 off-season, she bought a baby grand piano and has been taking private lessons ever since!

6.   Join a group of writers, artists, musicians, or whatever your passion is this year.

7.   Attend readings, lectures, workshops, conferences, demonstrations, and trade shows in the fields you're interested in learning more about.

8.   Volunteer in an area of avocational interest. For example, if you like teaching, volunteer to teach at your synagogue or Sunday school.

9.   Work part time at a job that intrigues you. Supplement your full-time employment with part-time work in an area of passion. For example, usher for the local theater, ballet, or symphony one night a week or volunteer to walk dogs for your local SPCA once each weekend.

10. Do something every day related to your passion. Examples:
     ❖   If you'd like to be a chef, cook a new gourmet meal once a week and read cooking books and recipes.
     ❖   If you'd like to be a gardener, plant and maintain a small garden (herbs are a good way to start).
     ❖   If you'd like to be a sailor, read books on sailing and go out once a week or take a class at your university extension.
     ❖   If you'd like to be a river guide, read, study and go rafting regularly.
     ❖   If you'd like to run a marathon, run four to five miles each day and 10 to 15 miles on the weekends.
     ❖   If you'd like to bicycle across the country, train in the gym and your garage and in your neighborhoods and local trails daily.

11.   Buy a 17 × 22 poster board and glue stick. Cut or tear photographs and words out of old magazines. Arrange and glue the words and photos on the board. This becomes your "wish board," (Gawain, 1977). Put the board up where only you will see it. Picture what you want. In my experience, everything on my wish boards have come true in some fashion within three months of creating them.

12.   If you want a change in your home environment— new house, new garden, remodeled kitchen—create a picture of it. I did this with a bathroom remodel and found a picture of what I wanted and, *voilà*, the bathroom is now transformed into my picture.

13.   If you're having trouble finding out what your heart's work would be, take out a blank sheet of paper and turn it horizontally. In the center, write *Heart's Work* and circle it. Now, free associate in all directions on the page, circling every word that comes to mind, no matter how ridiculous or unrelated it seems. This "right-brain clustering" exercise (Rico, 2000) can really help you uncover your native talents.

14.   Create a pie chart of your typical workday. Then assess: Is more than 50 percent of your day spent doing what you love? What percent of your day is currently spent doing what you love? How can you increase that percentage in your current circumstances? In another job within your organization? In another company?

15.   Take out a blank sheet of paper and number it one through five. Answer the question, "What would I do even if nobody paid me to do it?" This will give you a major clue into where you are now and what you'd like to be doing.

Chapter 12

*When you hit the glass ceiling,
move to another room.*

The CEO

*Life is what we make it.
Always has been, always will be.*

~ Grandma Moses
American Primitive painter

Rags to Riches

She started out dirt poor in rural Mississippi. She lived with her grandmother on a farm until she was six years old, then abruptly had to move to Milwaukee to live with her mother. At age 13, she was sent to a juvenile detention home for running away from abuse and molestation. The only reason she was not incarcerated was that they didn't have enough beds in the facility at the time. So, at age 13, she was again uprooted and sent, as a last resort, to live with her stern father,

Vernon, in Nashville, Tennessee. One of his rigors required her to read a book and write a book report every week. That early discipline may have formed the foundation for her lifelong love of reading.

She had a dream of becoming a broadcast journalist and got her chance at age 17 when she was hired by WVOL Radio in Nashville. In two years, she signed on with WTVF-TV as a reporter/anchor and quickly moved to Baltimore, where she co-anchored WJZ-TV's *People Are Talking*. In 1984, a floundering Chicago talk show, *AM Chicago,* hired her as anchor and soon was renamed *The Oprah Winfrey Show*. The rest is history. Oprah's show became the number one talk show in national syndication in less than one year, and won three Daytime Emmy Awards in 1987. In 1988, her own production company, Harpo Productions, Inc., acquired ownership and all production rights for *The Oprah Winfrey Show,* making Oprah the first woman in history to own and produce her own talk show. In 2003, Oprah became the first African-American woman to become a billionaire, noted in *Forbes* list of American billionaires.

Controlling production, Oprah has taken control of her own destiny, as well. It's a well-known fact that most women are forced to leave television at age 40, while men can work until they choose to leave the air, paunchy, balding, and aging well past 60 still on camera. Women, let alone African-American women, rarely make it in front of the network television cameras, but Oprah not only made it, she paved the way for other non-Hollywood types, including Martha Stewart. Who would have thought a kitchen show would make it big in American television back when Stewart started in her apron and rubber gloves? By controlling her own programming, Oprah has been able to raise more significant issues, make more best-selling authors, and distribute more wealth than possibly any other television personality in history.

From car giveaways to foundations to help AIDS victims in Africa, Oprah's influence is felt. More African-Americans, and Americans in general, are reading more literature than ever before directly due to Oprah's inauguration of the Oprah Book Club, which has kept mothers and grandmothers reading for the past 10 years. (Parents and grandparents are the biggest influencers of their children's literacy.) Her efforts on behalf of the passage of the National Child Protection Act were so significant, the convicted child abuser registry bill was dubbed the "Oprah Bill" and signed into law by President Clinton in 1993. No Jerry Springer, the maven of sensation, Oprah knew that network television would never sponsor a book club, host a talk show on domestic violence, or educate an entire population of women on the importance of breast cancer screenings. Rather than spend years bucking the system and banging her head against a glass ceiling, Oprah drew up her own plans and both starred in and produced her own talk show, regularly ranked number one and winner of numerous Emmy and other awards. Not everyone has the drive Oprah has, but every woman always has the option: When you hit the glass ceiling, move to another room.

The Odds Aren't Great

Although women hold 50.3 percent of all management and professional positions, they still hold only 1.6 percent of the CEO positions, and 7.9 percent of the top earner slots in the Fortune 500. With Carly Fiorina's departure in early 2005, there are now only eight women CEOs in the Fortune 500:

- ❖ Brenda Barnes, Sara Lee (#104)
- ❖ Mary F. Sammons, Rite Aid (#128)
- ❖ Anne M. Mulcahy, Xerox (#130)
- ❖ Patricia F. Russo, Lucent (#243)

❖ Andrea Jung, Avon Products (#275)
❖ S. Marce Fuller, Mirant (#314)
❖ Eileen Scott, Pathmark Stores (#432)
❖ Marion O. Sandler, Golden West Financial Corp. (#440)

None have cracked the Fortune 100, let alone the Fortune 50.

Though women comprise 35 percent of MBA students, a Catalyst study showed that only 13.6 percent are members of Fortune 500 board of directors (*Catalyst*, 2005). The Department of Labor statistics show that women earn 77 cents or less on the dollar to men, consistently lower earnings than men over the past 20 years, despite breakthroughs in education, legislation, and experience on the job.

There's a global glass ceiling, too. Even though 80 percent of human resources executives polled said that global experience is increasingly a must for advancement in large corporations, only 13 percent of the middle managers posted overseas by U.S. corporations were women. Despite stereotypes that women prefer to stay in one place, of the frequent flyers— men and women who travel overseas—surveyed by Catalyst, 47 percent of women said they would be willing to relocate overseas within the year, compared with 51 percent of men (*Catalyst*, 2000).

Ironically, despite all the studies that show financial performance is higher for companies with more women at the top, senior executives have failed to take note of the startling results of one of the many studies of 353 of the Fortune 500 companies that demonstrated that companies with the highest representation of women on their senior management teams had a 35 percent higher return on equity and a 34 percent higher total return to shareholder value that those with the lowest women's representation (*Catalyst*, 2004).

Why Women Leave

Job dissatisfaction issues are most often cited among women entrepreneurs. Cromie and Hayes (1988) found factors such as dissatisfaction, frustration, and boredom in previous jobs as the most frequently cited reasons for pursuing entrepreneurship. Using a five-point Likert-type scale, Cromie and Hayes found that women entrepreneurs most frequently cite limitations for mobility at their job, that is, glass ceiling issues, as motivation for self-employment.

General Electric, a stellar 20-year growth and earnings producer, counts only 13.8 percent women among its corporate officers, despite an average of 15.7 percent for all the Fortune 500 companies. A leader of one of the 20 businesses that provided 90 percent of GE's earnings in 1999, Sandra Derickson, heading up the GE Capital Auto Financial Services' line of business, left unceremoniously in 1999 after the fast-growing auto-leasing unit posted a sharp earnings decline. A man replaced her. Anne Poirson, a computer scientist and former GE systems designer, said, "Someone in my position is not going to stick around at GE and wait for equality to simmer through the corporation. Yes, it's a very good company, but in my particular case, I didn't think it was going to pay off for me." Poirson resigned in 1986 after five years with the company to go into business for herself. She, at 52, feels her software consulting company gives her more control over her career (*SF Chronicle*, November 20, 2005). At the system-wide University of California, only 25.1 percent of faculty hires for academic year 1999-2000 were women. The U.C. Berkeley math department has not hired a female faculty member in nine years!

Why do the best and the brightest leave Corporate America after just five years? More than half the Stanford women MBAs leave Corporate America to start their own businesses within five years of getting their graduate degrees (Carol Bartz, Stanford Executive Breakfast, 1996). The realization by the most educated and senior-level women that their corporate futures are limited becomes apparent soon after graduation.

White males who run most of Corporate America still want to do business with the "good old boys" they know. *The Glass Ceiling Report* (1995) found that 97 percent of senior managers of Fortune 1000 industrial and Fortune 500 firms were white men (Glass Ceiling Report, U.S. Department of Labor, 1995). Men cut deals on the golf courses that women are excluded from during certain hours. Their "club" is governed by backroom deals, barroom conversations, and the ubiquitous sports analogies that leave most women out.

Judy Rosener, management professor at UC-Irvine and author of *America's Competitive Secret: Women Managers* (1997), believes you can't break the glass ceiling from below: "You'll get blood in your face and glass in your eyes." Instead, she says you have to remove it from above: "The men who are up there must be convinced that it's in their own self-interest to remove that ceiling. But the women's glass ceiling is a floor for the men, and they may have a fear of falling" (Rosener, 1997).

I used to think that the military or football would have been good training for me as a woman in business. I would have been wrong, of course. There's a reason the military closes ranks and a reason football is mostly closed to women. A lot goes on in the trenches and locker rooms that binds men to one another and keeps women out.

Corporate America is similar. The only morality is profit and growth. In the military, it's winning wars. In sports, it's winning games. As Vince Lombardi said, "Winning isn't everything. It's the only thing!" This is a concept lost on most women who value relationships over results and cooperation over competition.

It Could Cost You Your Life

The price to break through the mahogany doors of the boardroom is high. A woman who succeeds in this world often surrenders soft pastels for harsh navy blues and bitter grays. The soft lines of the feminine are replaced with the sharp edges of the spreadsheet and the stiff upper lip of the executive suite. The assault on women does not end here. Women learn to put on a "game face" that keeps their emotions down.

Where do those emotions go? Often, they thud down the esophagus, lodging in the colon or struggling through the system, building up within like some toxic waste dump. Sometimes, the feelings get caught in the throat, stuck in the sternum, or strangled around the heart. That's one reason why women are not only one of the fastest-growing segments of heart attack sufferers, but also more often die from their first heart attack than do men. Heart disease remains the leading cause of death for women older than age 45 in the United States. According to the American Heart Association, women are more than 12 times more likely to die from heart disease than from breast cancer. Women, more often than men, die from cardiovascular disease: nearly 500,000 a year, in fact (American Heart Association, 2005). The constriction of feeling wraps around the aorta and can literally kill the very drive that propels women ahead. The Type A behavior (Friedman, 1985) that often is a precursor to heart attacks is easy to spot: multitasking, impatience, and perfectionism.

Check yourself for these symptoms before it's check-out instead of check-in time.

In the Bedroom or the Boardroom: Women Lose

Many women take another route to the top (it still goes on, trust me): They wear flaming red lipstick and sport perfect acrylic nails. Their silk blouses with plunging necklines and open-toed high-heel shoes lead them into the affections of their male colleagues. In fact, their attractiveness and seductive wiles are the only calling cards they bring into the executive suite. This path to power alienates them from other professional women and makes them a target of scurrilous gossip throughout the organization. Like any affair, it is often short-lived. Once the executive captures his prey, the game is over. Usually, it is the woman who loses. Even former President Bill Clinton got off relatively free for his dalliance with his White House intern, Monica Lewinsky. The worst part of acquiring power by "sleeping your way to the top" or implying that you would is that women who succeed this way are left with low self-esteem and very few friends in the company. Who's going to confide in the gal sleeping with the boss?

Boardroom interactions go against everything women have learned about communication. Sensitivity, attentiveness, cooperation, and warmth are replaced with jockeying for power, insensitive joking, scant listening, competition, and nasty outflanking maneuvers. Forced gaiety often masks deep hostilities and major power struggles. The foray usually begins with a round of put-downs of disenfranchised groups not present and ends with pointed and personal attacks.

Hitting the glass ceiling can do more than give you a headache; it could give you a permanent head injury. Trying to push a culture that seeks to limit and quiet your voice can have dire consequences for your health. Isolating yourself in your rise to the top can leave you lonely and broken. A promotion in a male-dominated workplace may cause a woman to feel as if she has to play by male rules. Unfortunately, this can backfire when dealing with female colleagues or subordinates, as observed in the book, *In the Company of Women: Turning Workplace Conflict into Powerful Alliances* (Heim et al., 2001). Trying to get into a club that doesn't want you can leave you feeling rejected and left out and not as good as you really are. It's a choice. Even if you do get in to the boardroom, if you're the only one, how comfortable, connected, and welcome will you feel on a daily basis? Are you really prepared for the pressures at the executive level when all your fellow male, and sometimes female, executives may be working against you?

Move to Another Room

Why not spare yourself the heartache and pain? Why not, upon encountering the last hurdle to the executive suite, the glass and, often, cement ceiling, move to another room? Better yet, why not build your own building?

Bright, creative women are leaving corporations and starting their own businesses in record numbers. The fastest-growing segment of small business owners across America is women. The number of women-owned businesses continues to grow at nearly twice the rate of all U.S. firms. Between 1997 and 2004, the number of women-owned firms in the United States increased 17 percent. Women-owned firms employ 19.1 million people and generate $2.5 trillion in sales, while spending an estimated $103 billion a year (Center for Women's Business Research, 2005).

Janet Hanson, for example, didn't set out to start her own firm. She was perfectly happy at Goldman, Sachs & Co. as the vice president and co-manager of money market sales (its first woman sales manager) and then as vice president of marketing for Goldman Sachs Asset Management. However, after she took time off to have her two children, upward mobility appeared blocked. "My only option? To start my own firm," says Hanson, who started Milestone Capital Management (*Workforce*, September 2000).

Working Less and Loving It More

In the Stanford Values and Lifestyles (VALS) scale, an analytical marketing tool developed by Stanford Research International (SRI) and sold to Fortune 500 companies, SRI found that only 1 percent of the population fell into the "actualizers" top of its five-tier model that sorted psychographic segmentation by values and lifestyles and divided the groups into status seekers, action-oriented, socially conscious, and bottom-tier strugglers. The actualizers combined high achievement and fulfillment with high resources. In fact, the original studies showed that the top 1 percent (originally called "integrated") made more money than all the other 99 percent combined. They tended to be self-employed and worked fewer hours (less than 20 hours a week) than any of the other market segments. Many women are opting out of the corporate route to success altogether and pursuing "their own thing." Many find they work less hours and make more money than they ever did trying to storm the executive suites of the Fortune 500 (*www.erg.sri.com*).

Consulting from home gives many women maximum flexibility, whether it's time with their children or time to go to the gym, time with the dog or time with friends, time alone or time with a partner. Contractors are hired for their expertise and delivery of quick results. Thus, politics are kept to a minimum and personal freedom at a maximum. Self-employment affords more write-offs of home office, books, computers, cars, phones, meals, and entertainment than salaried employment. These write-offs allow you, as an entrepreneur, to keep most of what you earn.

Follow the Money

Only 5 percent of venture capital goes to women and many venture funds have never considered a proposal by women. Female entrepreneurs cite a number of barriers to getting venture capital, including an absence of developed business networks, a basic lack of business experience, and gender bias. That's why the Women's Venture Capital Forum sponsored "Springboard 2000 Bootcamp." Out of a pool of 300 applicants, 25 women were selected. The first two forums, held in Silicon Valley and Washington, DC, raised more than $200 million in venture capital for selected women. Ginger Lew, of the Telecommunications Development Fund, found that women tend to be overprepared and less willing to take a chance on a concept. Sometimes, that can mean missed opportunities. "People are comfortable with people they hang out with. Traditionally, male dominated bastions have perpetuated themselves," Oliver Curme of BatteryVentures in Wellesley admitted (*San Francisco Chronicle*, 2000). So, if you want to "use other people's money" as all the entrepreneurial pundits advise, find out more about the Women's Venture Capital Forum based in Boston, and Small Business Administration loans earmarked for women. It's not easy starting a business, but it's a lot easier starting a business with sufficient capital.

Money Is Not the Only Measure of Success

Money isn't the only measure of success. In fact, many self-employed women give up lucrative salaries and broad benefits packages to earn half or less of what they've earned at the peak of their careers. There can be no price tag on your time, however. Once it's gone, you never get it back. It's like the MasterCard commercials that list all the things money can buy, then close with, "Time with your children: priceless."

Trading time and barter for money can be lucrative, too. One small business owner I know publishes a directory of small businesses south of Market Street in San Francisco. She often gets "trades" of gym memberships, restaurant dinners, and museum tickets as part of her payment and lives quite luxuriously on a modest income. She makes all her own dishes and cups in the pottery classes she's taken during the past 12 years. She's tiled her own kitchen and bathroom and even put in her own hardwood floors. She makes pottery gifts and cooks from scratch. When she's low on cash, she brings apple pies made from her apple tree to dinner parties. Her life is rich, though her tax returns are modest.

Another woman creates corporate videos with Oscar-winning film studios. She takes a theater jaunt to New York every year and even has time to cover a booth at the Women's Craft Fair for her son's private school. She's always worried about her next gig, but loves what she does and wouldn't trade the security for the stimulation ever.

With self-employment, you determine the rules. You set the goals. If you want more time and balance, you devise a plan to make that happen. If you want higher income, you charge more for your services or hire lower-paid employees and derive the profits from good management. With self-employment, the ceiling is the sky. And the sky's the limit!

Room with a Different View

Don't trade one pair of handcuffs for another. Many women suffer from the "can't say no" syndrome. This self-sabotaging behavior doesn't change when you become self-employed. In fact, it might be exacerbated by the desperate push for success. Moving to another room means changing the way you view success.

Success could mean working nine months out of the year as a schoolteacher, taking long trips every summer vacation, and being home when your kids get out of school every day. Success can be working three months on and three months off. Women who work part time (35 hours or less a week) made up 26 percent of all female wage and salary workers in 2004 (U.S. Department of Labor, Women's Bureau, 2004). Success could also entail working half time for a nonprofit and half time for yourself, or working part time in a corporation and pursuing a hobby the rest of the time.

Whether baking biscotti or writing a book, building a business or acting on a lifelong dream, move to another room, one with your own view.

If you're constantly stymied by the obstacles posed while climbing the corporate ladder and if the glass ceiling feels impenetrable, step back and consider a move to another room. Become the CEO of your own company. Long before women worked for corporations, Virginia Woolf advised that every woman needs "a room of one's own" (Woolf, 1929).

There is no corporate ladder when you're CEO. You're in charge. You hold the keys to all the doors. The design is yours. The foundation is already in place. The subcontractors have already been paid along the corporate road you left. You've obtained all the right permits.

The only approval you're waiting for is your own.

Exercises

1. Take this test to see if you're ready for self-employment:

    ❖   Is there something you would love to do even if no one paid you to do it?
    ❖   Do you have at least a year's salary (preferably, two years' salary) in reserve that you're willing to gamble on a business venture?
    ❖   Could you get a job if your business venture failed?

    If you answer yes to all three questions, explore the possibilities of self-employment.

2. What would you do if you had no time or age constraints?

3. What work have you earned a salary for? (Maybe a client would be willing to pay you for that service if you contracted it out.)

4. Are you the kind of person who never has enough time and is never bored? You may have the personality for the self-motivation required for self-employment.

5. If you did not have a structured, salaried job, how would you spend your day? Maybe you have the self-discipline for self-employment.

6. What tasks have you been able to discipline yourself to do without any outside push:

- ❖ Plant and harvest a garden.
- ❖ Remodel a house.
- ❖ Play an instrument.
- ❖ Restore furniture.
- ❖ Paint a house.
- ❖ Write a book.
- ❖ Obtain a college degree while working full time.
- ❖ Run a marathon.
- ❖ Obtain a certification.
- ❖ Master a foreign language.

Can you take one of these avocations and turn it into a money-making proposition?

7. Do you work to live (like the Europeans) or live to work? (Yes to the first question is a positive indicator.) Do you look forward to weekends and holidays or do you dread them? (Yes to the first question is a clue.)

8. Do your title and your salary determine your worth? (No is the right answer.)

9. Do you have a special talent that you can turn into at least a part-time, moneymaking venture? (One writer I know teaches writing in the public schools and runs writing workshops several times a year.)

10. Are you a good money manager? Do you keep as much or more than you spend? Suze Orman (2000/ 1997) says that it's not what you make, but how much you *keep* that counts.

11. Are you doing what you came here to do? Have you found your mission in life? If not, consider taking a workshop in finding your mission and creating your

vision statement for your life. A vision should be larger than yourself, make the world a better place, and be lifelong work and have the pull of a calling.

12. Explore the prospects for self-employment by reading books and attending seminars on the topic.

13. Talk to all the self-employed people you know about what they do and how they do it.

14. Take inventory to determine your interests and predilections.

15. Hire a career coach and explore your suitability for self-employment, part-time employment, or nonprofit employment.

16. Take a free Small Business Administration class.

17. Go to a conference for women entrepreneurs.

18. Read professional and business owner newsletters and attend conferences.

19. Attend your local businesswomen's breakfasts or lunches.

20. Save a year's salary to afford you maximum flexibility in deciding what room you want to be in for the rest of your life.

Conclusion

*Remember, you can have it all.
Just not all at once.*

Notes

Introduction

National Association of Female Executives. 2005.
www.nafe.com.

Hochschild, Arlie, Ph.D., with Anne Machung. *The Second Shift.* New York: Penguin Group, 2003.

Hewlett, Sylvia Ann. *Creating a Life: Professional Women and the Quest for Children.* New York: Hyperion, 2002.

Greer, Germaine. *The Whole Woman.* London/New York: Doubleday/Random House; Knopf/Random House. Anchor Books/Random House, 2000.

Guiliano, Mireille. *French Women Don't Get Fat: The Secret of Eating for Pleasure.* New York: Knopf Publishing Group, 2004.

Durand, Martine, Deputy Director and Sonnet, Anne, Labour Economist, Directorate for Employment, Labour and Social Affairs. "France: Jobs and Older Workers," Organization for Economic Cooperation and Development. *www.oecdobserver.org,* October 2005.

Ackman, Dan. "France, Bastion of Productivity." Forbes.com. *www.forbes.com,* March 2005.

Chapter 1 ❖ The Princess

National Association for Executive Women. Issue on top 30 companies for executive women, 2004.

Working Mother's Best Lists, annually.

Moskowitz, Milton, and Levering, Robert. *Best 100 Companies to Work for in America,* new list published in *Fortune* magazine bi-annually.

National Association for Executive Women. "Top 30 Companies for Executive Women," 2004.

Professional Businesswomen of California Conference. Every May in the San Francisco Bay Area.

Working Mother. "100 Best Companies for Women." Published every October.

Working Mother. "Best Companies for Women of Color." First issue focused on Women of Color published in 2003.

Guide to WorkLife Quality. PriceWatershouseCoopers employee handbook.

Jung, Andrea. CEO of Avon Products, featured. *www.goldsea.com,* January 1998.

Catalyst Report. "The Bottom Line: Corporate Performance and Gender Diversity." *www.catalystwomen.org,* January 2004.

Chapter 2 ❖ The Soccer Mom

Babcock, Linda, Ph.D. and Laschever, Sara. *Women Don't Ask: Negotiation and the Gender Divide.* New Jersey: Princeton University Press, 2003.

Expedia.com. "Expedia.com Survey Reveals that American Workers Are Estimated to Leave More Than 421 Million Vacation Days on the Table in 2005." May 2005.

Hochschild, Arlie, Ph.D. *The Second Shift.* New York: Penguin Group, 2003.

Cedars, Marcelle, M.D., Director of the University of California San Francisco Center for Reproductive Health. "The Biological Clock." CBSNews.com, 2003.

Hewlett, Sylvia Ann. *Creating a Life: Professional Women and the Quest for Children.* New York: Hyperion, 2002.

Harrow, Susan. *Sell Yourself without Selling Your Soul: A Woman's Guide to Promoting Herself, Her Business, Her Product or Her Cause with Integrity and Spirit.* New York: HarperCollins Publishers, Inc., 2002.

Briskin, Alan. *The Stirring of Soul in the Workplace.* San Francisco: Jossey-Bass, Inc., a Wiley Company, 1996.

Ponder, Catherine. *The Prospering Power of Love.* Missouri: Unity, 1966.

Cameron, Julia. *The Artist's Way: A Spiritual Path to Higher Creativity.* Los Angeles: Jeremy Tarcher, Perigee Publishing Group, 1992.

Sher, Barbara. *I Could Do Anything If I Only Knew What It Was: How to Discover What You Really Want and How to Get It.* New York: Dell Trade Paperback, 1994.

Sher, Barbara. *Creating Your Second Life After 40.* Rocky Mountain Public Broadcasting Video, 1998.

Chapter 3 ❖ The Psychic

McCartney, Paul (lyrics) and Lennon, John (composer). "All You Need Is Love," 1967.

Wood, Grant. *American Gothic.* Art Institute of Chicago, 1930.

Moskowitz, Milton and Levering, Robert. *The 100 Best Companies to Work for in America.* New York: Penguin Books, 1993.

Carnegie, Dale. *How to Win Friends and Influence People.* New York: Simon and Schuster, Inc., 1981.

Chapter 4 ❖ The Socialite

Prince. "Party Like It's 1999," 1982.

U.S. Department of Labor. *The Glass Ceiling Report,* 1995.

Goleman, Daniel. *Emotional Intelligence: Why it can matter more than IQ.* New York: Bantam, 1995.

www.sybase.com. cited from Harvard University Study with Bain & Company, 1995.

www.e.i.haygroup.com, EQ studies based on Daniel Goleman's work. Bantam, 1995.

Woo, Suzanne. *On Course for Business: Women and Golf.* New York: John Wiley & Sons, 2002.

Business Week. "Belizean Grove." February 2001.

Weill, Andrew, M.D. *8 Weeks to Optimum Health.* New York: Knopf, 1997.

Math, Education and Science Achievement. *www.mesa.ucop.edu*

Chapter 5 ❖ The Diva

Babcock, Linda, Ph.D. and Laschever, Sara. *Women Don't Ask: Negotiation and the Gender Divide.* New Jersey: Princeton University Press, 2003.

Chapter 6 ❖ The Cheerleader

Neil, Randy and Hart, Elaine. *The Official Cheerleader's Handbook.* New York: Fireside, 1986.

Professional Businesswomen of California Conference. San Francisco, May 2004.

Thompson, Jim. *Positive Coaching Alliance.* Stanford University. 2005.

Gottman, John, Ph.D. *Marriage Studies.* Washington: *www.uwnews.org,* 1994.

Nicholls. *Positive Coaching Alliance.* Stanford University, 1984.

DeAngelis, Barbara and Chopra, Deepak, M.D. *Relationships as a Bridge to Divine Love.* Carlsbad: Hay House Audiocassette, 2001.

Chapter 7 ❖ The Girl Scout

The Girl Scout Promise. *www.girlscouts.org*

The Girl Scout Law. *www.girlscouts.org*

Business Ethics "2004 100 Best Corporate Citizens." November, 2005.

Stills, Stephen. "Love the One You're With," 1970.

American Heart Association. *www.americanheart.org,* 2005.

Friedman, Meyer, M.D. *Type A Behavior and Your Heart.* New York: Fawcett Crest, 1985.

Bloomfield, Harold, M.D., Cain, Michael, Jaffe, Dennis and Kory, Robert. *TM.* New York: Dell Publishing, 1975.

Lee, I-Min and Paffenbarger, Ralph. "College Alumni Health Study." Harvard University, October 1998.

Moskowitz, Milton and Levering, Robert. *The 100 Best Companies to Work for in America.* New York: Penguin Books, 1993.

Chapter 8 ❖ The Apprentice

Trump, Donald. *The Apprentice.*

U.S. Department of Labor. *The Glass Ceiling Report*, 1995.

Catalyst Report. "Women in Leadership: Comparing European and U.S. Women Executives," 1996.

National Association of Female Executives. *www.nafe.com,* 2005.

Steinem, Gloria. Pacific Institute Address on Aging Gracefully. San Francisco, December 2, 2004.

Evans, Joan, Ph.D. and Avis, Susan, Ed. D. *The Women Who Broke All the Rules: How the Choices of a Generation Changed Our Lives.* Illinois: Sourcebooks, Inc., 1999.

Evans, Joan, Ph.D. and Avis, Susan, Ed.D. Presentation, "Dream Big and Think Smart: The Power of Personal Planning." San Francisco Bay Area, 2003.

Management Mentors. *www.managment-mentors.com,* 2004.

www.hr.com

Woo, Suzanne. *On Course for Business: Women and Golf.* New York: John Wiley & Sons, 2002.

Professional Businesswomen of California. Annual conferences. *www.pbwc.org*

Chapter 9 ❖ The Chef

Child, Julia. *www.pbs.org*

Pepin, Jacques. *www.jacquespepin.net*

Babcock, Linda, Ph.D. and Laschever, Sara. *Women Don't Ask: Negotiation and the Gender Divide.* New Jersey: Princeton University Press, 2003.

Waters, Alice. Executive Chef and Owner, *Chez Panisse* restaurant owner since 1971. *www.chezpanisse.com*

Remen, Rachel, M.D. *Kitchen Table Wisdom: Stories That Heal.* New York: Riverhead, 1996.

Kawasaki, Guy. *The Art of the Start: The Time-Tested, Battle-Hardened Guide for Anyone Starting Anything.* New York: Portfolio Hardcover, 2004.

Babcock, Linda, Ph.D. and Laschever, Sara. *Women Don't Ask: Negotiation and the Gender Divide.* New Jersey: Princeton University Press, 2003.

Nassif, Sr. Rosemarie, Ph.D. *www.hnu.edu,* 2005.

Ram Dass. *Be Here Now.* New York: Crown Publishers, 1971.

Ram Dass. *Still Here: Embracing Aging, Changing and Dying.* NY: Riverhead Books, 2000.

Chapter 10 ❖ The Athlete

Covey, Stephen. *The 7 Habits of Highly Effective People.* New York: Fireside, 1989.

Collins, Jim. *Good to Great: Why Some Companies Make the Leap...and Others Don't.* New York: HarperCollins Publishers, Inc., 2001.

Johnson, Spencer. *The Present: The Gift That Makes You Happier and More Successful At Work and In Life, Today!* New York: Doubleday, 2003.

www.cefe.org/acve. On portfolio workers.

diPaolo, Andy, Ph.D., Executive Director. Center for Professional Development. Senior Associate Dean Engineering. Stanford University, 2001.

Center for Disease Control. *www.cdc.gov,* 2005.

Hochschild, Arlie, Ph.D.,with Anne Machung. *The Second Shift.* New York: Penguin Group, 2003.

Orman, Suze, *9 Steps to Financial Freedom.* New York: Three Rivers Press/Crown Publishers, 2000/1997.

"Thrive." Kaiser Ad Campaign. 2005.

Veal, Debra. PBWC Conference. San Francisco, May 4, 2004.

Rockne, Knute (1888-1931) in *15th Edition of Bartletts Familiar Quotaions.* New York: Little Brown and Company, Inc., 1980.

Chapter II ❖ The Soul Sister

Goldberg, Whoopi. *www.imdb.com/whoopi.goldberg*

Packer, ZZ. *Drinking Coffee Elsewhere.* New York: Riverhead, 2003.

Sher, Barbara. *Wishcraft: How to Get What You Really Want.* New York: Ballantine Books, 1983.

Sher, Barbara. *Creating Your Second Life After 40.* Rocky Mountain Public Broadcasting Video, 1998.

Galán, Nely. PBWC Conference Keynote Address. San Jose, May 2003.

Briskin, Alan. *The Stirring of Soul in the Workplace.* San Francisco: Jossey-Bass, Inc., a Wiley Company, 1996.

Ponder, Catherine. *Prospering Power of Love.* Missouri: Unity, 1966.

Crewe, Bob and Nolan, Kenny. "Lady Marmalade," 1997.

Gawain, Shakti. *25ᵗʰ Anniversary Edition of Creative Visualization.* New York: Bantam New Age Books, 2002.

Rico, Gabrielle, Ph.D., *Writing the Natural Way.* New York: Jeremy P. Tarcher/Putnam, 2000.

Chapter 12 ❖ The CEO

Winfrey, Oprah. *Oprah.com*

Catalyst Report. "Women MBAs." *www.catalystwomen.org,* October 2005.

Catalyst Report. "Passport to Opportunity: U.S. Women in Global Business," 2000.

Catalyst Report. "The Bottom Line: Corporate Performance and Gender Diversity." *www.catalystwomen.org,* January 2004.

Cromie, S. and Hayes, J. "Towards a typology of female entrepreneurs." University of Pretoria, South Africa, 1988.

Derickson, Sandra. Forbes.com, November 2005.

Bartz , Carol. Stanford Executive Breakfast, 1996.

U.S. Department of Labor. *The Glass Ceiling Report*, 1995.

Rosener, Judy B., Ph.D. *America's Competitive Secret: Women Managers.* London: Oxford University Press, 1997.

American Heart Association. *www.americanheart.org,* 2005.

Heim, Patricia, Ph.D., Murphy, Susan, Ph.D. and MBA, with Golant, Susan K. *In the Company of Women: Turning Workplace Conflict into Powerful Alliances.* New York: Jeremy Tarcher, 2001.

Center for Women's Business Research. *www.nfwbo.org,* 2005.

Workforce. September 2000.

www.erg.sri.com/its/sri_c/rpt3_1.pdf . Stanford Values and Lifestyles scale.

San Francisco Chronicle. "Women's Venture Capital Forum," October 2000.

U.S. Department of Labor Women's Bureau. 2004.

Woolf, Virginia. *A Room of One's Own.* London: Harcourt, Inc., 1929.

Index

❖ 217 ❖

Booz Allen Hamilton, 21
Briskin, Alan, 38, 176
Brown, Kathleen, 26
Buddhist, 130, 137
    dharma, 173
Bullock, Sandra, 99
Bush, George W., 75, 100
Business Ethics magazine, 116
Business Week magazine, 75
Bustamante, Sergio, 78
buying down, 39

C

Cage, Nicholas, 127
Cameron, Julia, 43
Carnegie Mellon University, 90
Carnegie, Dale, 54, 63, 99
Catmull, Dr. Ed, 127
Center for Women's
    Business Research, 193
Charles Schwab, 60, 76, 81, 122,
    134, 137, 154
Chevron Texaco, 21, 137
chi, balancing your, 42
Chicago Art Institute, 56
Child, Julia, 139
childcare, 22
choose your attitude, 164
Chopra, Deepak, 106
Cisco Systems, 76, 104
Citibank, 137
Citicorp, 75
Clausen, A.W., 75
Clinton, Bill, 187, 192
College of Prof. Studies, 81
Collins, Jim, 157
Color Purple, The, 170
Columbia Medical School, 51
Commonwealth Club, 121
control
    freaks, 95
    external lotus of, 96

Convention Center, 72
cook's tour, the, 140
Coors, Joseph, 75
Coppola, Francis Ford, 128
CoreStates, 56
Cornell University, 100
Corporate America, 35, 130,
    141, 189-190
corpus callosum, 52
Coughlin, Natalie, 155, 165
Couric, Katie, 100
Covey, Stephen, 157
credit report, giving a, 106
Cunningham, Merce, 128
Curme, Oliver, 195

D

Dalai Lama, the, 41, 141, 150
Dass, Ram, 150
Davenport, Lindsay, 161
DeAngelis, Barbara, 106
Deloitte & Touche, 26, 60
Diaz, Cameron, 100
Dickinson, Emily, 139
DiMarco, Stephanie, 155
diva, rules for becoming a, 96
Douglas, Michael, 100
Dragila, Stacey, 155
Drinking Coffee Elsewhere, 171
DUMBO arts district, 78

E

earthquake, the great, 16
eBay, 154
Eisenhower, Dwight D., 101
Emergency Preparedness
    Team, 118
emotional intelligence, 73
Employee Assistance Line, 37
Emporium, 17
EQ, 73

About the Author

From Silicon Valley icons to Fortune 500 CEOs, Kathleen Archambeau has coached, trained, taught, and worked with more than 20,000 corporate warriors across three continents, in seven countries, and 26 U.S. states. Her clients and customers have included the Bank of New York, Chemical Bank, Comerica, Deutsche Telekom, Ericsson, France Telecom, Genentech, Hewlett-Packard, the James River Corporation, Johnson & Johnson, Motorola, Sybase, Symantec, and Wells Fargo Bank. A university professor, Archambeau teaches organizational behavior at the University of San Francisco and helps working adults actualize their dreams. She lives with her beloved in the San Francisco Bay Area.